all the days after

A story of love, loss and resilience
beyond Black Saturday

SUE GUNNINGHAM

All the Days After

First published in 2015 in Australia and New Zealand by Finch Publishing Pty Limited,
ABN 49 057 285 248, Suite 2207, 4 Daydream Street, Warriewood, NSW, 2102, Australia.

ISBN: 978-0-6486646-0-4

Copyright © 2015 Sue Gunningham
Republished by Sue Gunningham 2019

The author asserts her moral rights in this work throughout the world without waiver. All rights reserved. No part of this publication may be reproduced, stored in a retrieval system or transmitted in any form or by any means (electronic or mechanical, through reprography, digital transmission, recording or otherwise) without the prior written permission of the publisher.

Edited by Jenny Scepanovic
Editorial assistance by Teaspoon Consultancy
Text typeset by Vicki McAuley
Cover design by Ingrid Kwong

Reproduction and Communication for educational purposes
The *Australian Copyright Act 1968* (the Act) allows a maximum of one chapter or 10% of the pages of this work, whichever is the greater, to be reproduced and/or communicated by any educational institution for its educational purposes provided that the educational institution (or the body that administers it) has given a remuneration notice to Copyright Agency Limited (CAL) under the Act. For details of the CAL licence for educational institutions contact: info@copyright.com.au

Profits from the sale of this book are donated with thanks to:
The Country Fire Authority
The Salvation Army
The Red Cross
The Centre for Grief and Bereavement
Their volunteers helped me through the hard times.

Contents

Part 1: Lost   1
Part 2: Stolen   106
Part 3: Examined   147
Part 4: Rebuild   203
Epilogue   267

On hearing of the loss of Barry
Burdened with longing, I went
To the forest at Waldene
to see my love,
To press him to my breast,
He; so bound to me
as it happened,
Me; whom he'd freed from bondage.
I found not the man, nor felt his presence.
I did not hear his forest either,
But I remember,
remember
to this day
How the policeman,
looking down at the ground
Said to me quietly, 'everything was burnt'
Everything went up in flames: his virtues and his vices
And the man,
and his cottage,
and his forest.
And there I stand before this hushed messenger
Quietly repeating:
burnt.

– Sue Gunningham, June 2011;
based on a poem by Boris Slutsky, translated by
Daniel Weissbort from a volume titled *Things That Happen*

PART 1

LOST

So we beat on, boats against the current, borne back ceaselessly into the past.

— *The Great Gatsby*. F. Scott Fitzgerald

1

And so it begins …

Monday 9 February 2009
The police officer told me to go back to my car and wait. I watched him through my windscreen. I had parked beside the road in this same location last night. The State Emergency Service (SES) men had prevented me from crossing the small bridge from where the road wound up through the hills beyond Humevale to Barry's cottage, Waldene. They had told me that the bridge pylons had been burnt and were no longer safe.

The fires had swept through unannounced and catastrophic on Saturday 7 February. I had kissed my tousled, sleepy-headed partner Barry goodbye when I left for work on that Saturday morning. I was to deliver a full-day curriculum inservice to a group of teachers in the city. Later, when I knocked off work at 4.30 pm, I had phoned him at Waldene to discuss our plans for the evening. During that brief phone call he told me that he was on alert in case of spot fires from the Wallan fire, which was about 15 km from Waldene, although he said that he could neither hear, see or smell any fire at that time.

Towards the end our five-minute conversation Barry suddenly went quiet. 'What's up?' I asked.

He hesitated a moment before answering, 'Nothing … I thought I heard something … maybe just the wind.' I could feel him straining to listen harder.

We decided that I would stay at the house where my office is located in Greensborough, about 25 kilometres from Waldene, for the night. Barry would stay at Waldene in case of spot fires. We hung up, not realising that within 30 minutes Barry would perish in the holocaust that was to become known as 'Victoria's Black Saturday'.

I was not overly concerned when I phoned the cottage three hours later to see how Barry was doing. The recorded message told me the line was temporarily unavailable. I assumed that the fires had brought a line down somewhere. I knew that Barry would eventually phone me or arrive in Greensborough when he was sure the cottage would be okay.

Mobile phone reception at the cottage is generally unreliable, often requiring a hike up to the roadside for even intermittent reception. As a result Barry had never owned a mobile phone. My job requires a mobile phone and I knew that Barry had that number as well as the landline number for the house at Greensborough, so he would have no trouble contacting me when he was ready.

At the Royal Commission hearing twelve months later, the arson chemist advised the Commissioners that the fire probably impacted Waldene between 5 and 5.05 pm on Black Saturday. This has left me with the unending task of trying to determine how Barry spent those precious 30 minutes between when he so calmly hung up the phone until he died. So many times in the years since the fire I have paced out various routes through the charred landscape, trying to imagine what happened. I stumble between burnt landmarks, from where the phone was located to the site of the fire bunker where he spent his last conscious moments.

Stopwatch in hand, I walk slowly, mimicking lack of oxygen; I run, mimicking fear. I have timed the drive down the road to where the first glimpse of fire on the ridge would have been visible, done a U-turn and sped back to the bunker; this because the police theorised that perhaps Barry had driven part way along the road to ascertain the source of the noise he thought he heard as we spoke on the phone. The more I pace and time my imaginings, the less I seem to know. Sometimes I lose sight of the purpose and instead merely seek solace from stepping wherever he might have stepped in those last 30 minutes.

I phoned the cottage again during that night, but always the recorded message advised me that the line was temporarily unavailable. What a cruel joke that message turned out to be. It provided an ignorant calm when the reality was that I had already lost Barry and all of our future. I look back now and wonder what I would have done if instead the recorded message had told me that Barry, Waldene, my life as I knew it, had all been destroyed. Perhaps I would not have had the strength to go on and only the forest would know the sweet secret that we lived and loved there.

Barry and I had first met in 1990 when we both were teaching at the same primary school. Our initial friendship developed into a romance and eventually deepened into love. The fact that we were both married to other people and that I had two young children meant that our relationship was kept secret from all but a few close friends. It was a decade later before we could live openly as a couple.

The sweltering night kept me awake at Greensborough. I listened to ABC Radio all night. The reports were about strange sounding towns and shires and regions; many of which I had never heard of before nor could place on the map. I heard reference to places that were unfamiliar: Murrindindi, Weerite, Coleraine, Yarra; an endless list of locations that must have existed beyond the major towns. I tried to check with the Country Fire Authority (CFA) about the status of Humevale but could not get through on the phone or internet. I listened for news about Whittlesea, not realising that for the sake of expediency the cottage had been, or later would be, grouped with the Kilmore East–Murrindindi reports even though the land falls under the jurisdiction of the City of Whittlesea.

I heard Kinglake referred to a few times on the radio, both via CFA information and through listeners phoning in. Kinglake is some 15 kilometres by road from Waldene. I later realised that the broadcasted calls from listeners may not have been indicative of the current situation at any time. There was no guarantee that a call was not a replay of an earlier recorded call or that the caller had not been hanging on the line for any amount of time or even that what they were saying was correct. In reality how many people are able to describe situations using compass directions correctly? Perhaps these call-ins may do more harm than good in times of crisis.

All night I listened to the radio. A male phoned in to describe what he could see from his backyard at Humevale. He described the fire in the hills behind his house bringing smoke and ash from the direction of Wallan. His report made me feel that Humevale had been spared. Humevale was apparently where people stood on their porches and watched the fire in the distance and rang the radio station for their three minutes of fame. It was not where the fires were actually burning.

Of course, later I found that the tiny township in the valley of Humevale was almost totally spared. The fire had instead roared across the hills behind, rushing upwards, ever upwards, consuming the forest and the cottage, and almost everything in its path towards Kinglake at the top of the range.

Sunday 8 February 2009

From early morning my phone began ringing as friends and relations from Victoria and interstate began checking to see if we were safe.

Some had phoned the cottage and received the 'line unavailable' message and then phoned my mobile. Those who did not know the cottage phone number had phoned my mobile directly after hearing the news broadcasts. Again and again, I explained the situation. I was sure that Barry would phone me as soon as he was able. I said I would have heard if there was a problem and that he was probably out patrolling the area around the cottage or helping wherever he might be needed. I was beginning to worry, but was not sure what I could do but wait.

My youngest son Blake and some of his friends were flying out to Bali later that night. They had organised to be picked up from the Greensborough house at 8 pm. Blake was aware that I was worrying about Barry but he kept telling me everything would be all right and that I was safer to remain at Greensborough than to drive towards any fires that may or may not be in the hills around Humevale. I listened to what he said, nodded in apparent agreement and then anxiously watched the hands of the clock drag slowly around to 8 pm. Finally I bundled the travellers into a car with a wave, a hasty 'goodbye' and the promise that I would 'not do anything silly'.

Almost before their car had turned the corner at the end of the street I was behind the steering wheel of my own car, reversing out of the driveway and heading for Whittlesea.

I was stopped by police at the Humevale Road turn-off on the Whittlesea–Yea Road. They were not allowing cars down the road because of smoke and spot fires up in the hills. I told the police about my concern for Barry. They were unsure how far along the ridge the fire was burning but they were not letting anyone along Humevale Road just in case.

I became distraught. I could not see the flames but even in

the darkness, the taste of smoke hung heavy in the air. I did not know what I could do. I could not phone or drive to the cottage. I considered the manner of the police at the roadblock. They had not appeared alarmed or frightened; more just doing their job, turning traffic away from a 'temporarily out-of-bounds road'.

The fact that the roadblock police did not necessarily know what catastrophe lay beyond the 'no-go' zone, but were told to just turn the traffic away, worked to their advantage. They were able to remain focused and diligent in their task. No-one received special treatment. They, like me, were unaware of what had occurred at Waldene.

I slowly drove back the 5 kilometres to Whittlesea. My mind was full of thoughts of how to get to the cottage and to find Barry wherever he was. I wondered if he might have decided to shelter in the fire bunker. This was the little underground 'room' he had built into the side of a hill just below the cottage. The fire was supposedly running up along the ridge of the hills. The cottage was down on the southern slope of the hill. Probably the fire would roar across the ridge on the northern side if it was heading towards Kinglake. If Barry was still at the cottage he might shelter in the bunker until the fire front had passed.

The bunker was a dark, creepy space about 3 metres square. It had rammed earth walls held back with metal pickets and sheets of corrugated iron. The roof was a large panel of metal along the lines of a discarded garage door. Barry had put a layer of concrete over this metal roof and then a layer of dirt that was planted with bright-eyed gazanias.

When Barry had first taken me to see the bunker years earlier I had laughingly dubbed it 'the bomb shelter' and lamented the fact that it lacked food or a toilet. I remember Barry smiled at my ignorance and explained that fire fronts go through quickly and that the bunker did not have to accommodate people for days but rather for minutes or perhaps an hour or two at most.

I later told the Royal Commission of this conversation when questioned about Barry's expectations of his bunker. Barry had built a fire bunker for protection against a grass or small scrub fire, little anticipating that no bunker yet invented would be able to withstand the holocaust that arrived on that February day in 2009.

By the time I had arrived back in Whittlesea I had convinced myself that if Barry was still at the property, he would in all likelihood be sheltering in the bunker. I drove slowly and aimlessly up and down the streets of the township trying to determine a course of action.

The fact that the bunker was underground meant that it was not immediately evident to anyone unfamiliar with the landscape at Waldene. In my mind's eye I considered the possibility of trees and debris falling across the bunker and Barry being trapped underground. I worried that if that happened he might perish before they allowed me onto the site to find him. The thought of him surviving a fire but dying because he was trapped underground was overwhelming.

I felt useless. I must do something. There was Barry and there was me. He would be relying on me. Inside my head I could hear my brain shrieking, 'Do something!'

Suddenly, with a sense of determination, I swung the car around and drove to the police station. The lights were on and there were a number of cars parked out the front. I sat in the car and drew a large map of the flat land at Waldene, marking in the long, steep driveway, the cottage, my writing studio, the small pond and the entry to the bunker. I labelled everything and marked approximate distances between the structures. I wrote my name and Barry's name on the sheet of paper along with the address of Waldene, the (out of service) phone number, my mobile number and the landline where I could be contacted in Greensborough.

I remember taking my place at the end of the queue that had formed in the narrow space from the door of the police station to the tiny counter where a lone police officer was trying to deal with many distraught residents as best he could. I waited my turn, feeling a rising tide of anxiety as the minutes ticked by. I had almost convinced myself by now that Barry was trapped under the ground in the bunker, absolutely dependent on me to send help or to come myself to rescue him.

Finally it was my turn to talk to the police officer on duty. I explained what I believed to be the case. I said that the roadblock police would not allow me into Humevale Road to get to the bunker. The police officer said that no-one was allowed past the roadblock. I showed him the map I had drawn. I started to cry. I pointed out all the features they should look for when they went searching. He took the map and listened to my explanations. He said he would get someone to check the bunker. He suggested that in the meantime I should go to the emergency station that had been set up at the Whittlesea Community Hall. He said that it was possible that I might even find Barry there and safe. Apparently lots of people had been evacuated from the hills to the community hall for protection.

I left the police station and drove to the community hall. There was a barricade across the road. I parked and wound down the window. A man stepped alongside the car and said no-one was allowed through. I began crying uncontrollably and said I could not find my partner and that the police had told me to come there.

I remember feeling a sort of rage that they were not letting people into the community hall, yet now, with hindsight, I think that the barricade was probably about stopping more cars coming into the parking area than actually stopping people going into the hall.

Probably all the man had meant was that I needed to park somewhere else and walk back to the hall. I became so upset that I could not stop crying long enough to explain myself clearly. Seeing the state I was in, the man kindly erred on the side of discretion, moved the barricade and waved me through. At last, a win in the battle to get to Barry.

I parked the car and pushed through the crowd of people milling around the outside of the centre. At the door Mrs Russell, the mother of a boy I had taught at primary school, came towards me. I think she was a volunteer helping to direct people to the myriad services available inside the hall. 'Hello, Sue,' she smiled in greeting. At the sight of a familiar face I began sobbing, this time sagging against her shoulder.

'I can't find Barry. I've tried everything but they won't let me through.' It is very likely that Mrs Russell had no idea who Barry was but to her credit she did not question me any further. With her arm around me she moved us over to a 'message wall' that had been set up for just this purpose. She found me a sticky note and pen and told me to write my phone number on the note along with a message. I wrote: Barry, phone Sue 04XXXXXXXX. Mrs Russell stuck the note onto the message board and explained to me that many people had been evacuated to various safe locations between Whittlesea and Kinglake.

She was quiet and calm and it was a great relief to be able to listen to her suggestion that Barry may be even now at one of those locations. The phone lines were down and it was difficult to get messages through at the moment. Mrs Russell said that if Barry came to this centre and had trouble remembering my phone number, it would be there waiting for him on the message board.

She took me into the main room of the community hall, saying we needed to move away from the doorway because journalists and photographers were already becoming a problem out the front of the building, taking photos and trying to interview people who were in great distress. Mrs Russell said that the police had banned photographers and journalists from entering the community hall. Her calm, sensible voice was very soothing and, feeling somewhat dazed, I went where she led me.

Along one wall of the room small tables had been positioned and behind each of these sat people wearing volunteer bibs. They were representatives from different church groups and the Red Cross. Mrs Russell steered me over to one of the tables and asked the man seated there if he could check the list of people who had been registered by the evacuation centres.

I gave the man Barry's details. He looked through a muddle of pages containing scribbled names and notes. I waited, perched on the edge of the seat, hoping that this man and his disorganised paperwork would finally locate Barry for me. The man could not find Barry's name in his lists. He assured me that the lists were far from complete. Unable to offer a resolution to my obvious grief, the man directed his comments to Mrs Russell. He suggested she take me to the table where they were registering missing people.

Mrs Russell led me away to where a grey-haired lady sat at a little table. She explained to the lady that I needed to register someone as missing. The lady gestured for me to sit down at her table. Mrs Russell gave me a parting hug and kindly, as though speaking to a child, she said that this lady would look after me now. I nodded and Mrs Russell moved away to resume her role at the front door of the building. I felt very much alone.

The grey-haired lady began to fill out a form. She said that her job was to collect information about missing people and that this information would be matched against the displaced people at the various evacuation centres. She began asking me a series of questions. When she asked my relationship to Barry I began crying uncontrollably. We were not legally married and I suddenly realised that the bureaucracy might therefore exclude me from receiving any information about his whereabouts. In my state I could not see a way around having to disclose that fact. It was too horrible.

The grey-haired lady sat quietly, making soothing noises. She asked if I wanted a cup of tea. I shook my head, sobbing and gasping for air. After a while, I calmed down enough to explain to the grey-haired lady.

'Barry and I aren't married; we have different surnames. But there's only me for Barry. There is no-one else. There's just us; just two.'

It was a series of fragmented words, spoken by a grief-stricken woman who was looking for her partner amidst a backdrop of noise and disaster and chaos.

The grey-haired woman leant over and patted my arm. 'I think we'll start the form again,' she said, ripping the partly completed document in half and throwing it in the bin. 'We'll say you're his wife,' she said. 'That way they will contact you when they find him.'

I remember the kindness of her words. I remember that she did not ask permission for her decision from anyone. Neither did she make me feel ashamed. She made no fuss. She was just a gentle, kindly, grey-haired lady who had volunteered to help and who did not need bureaucracy to tell her what was the right thing to do in this situation.

It was now after 11 pm. I walked slowly out of the community hall and got back into my car. There was still a crowd outside and lights had been erected to chase away the darkness. I sat in the car wondering what I should do now. I had been told that someone would phone me when Barry was located. I thought of him up at some evacuation centre higher up the hill. He would hate being unable to contact me. He would hate being ordered not to travel beyond the evacuation centre until he was given permission. He would be worrying about me worrying. I decided to go back to the house at Greensborough. At least that way I could be contacted on the landline and the mobile, just in case Barry rang.

The thought that he might even now be trying to phone me at Greensborough made me anxious to get back there. I was disappointed to find that no message had been left on the landline when I arrived. I sat next to the phone waiting. Beside me the ABC radio channel continued to give reports of fires burning in places with unfamiliar names.

The minutes ticked by. I felt a rising sense of panic. There must be something more that I could do. I began pacing, trying to think what was possible. What is the main thing? I asked myself. I reasoned that if the fire had burnt the cottage then Barry had either been evacuated or he would be in the bunker waiting to be rescued or he would be in the bunker waiting for the fire to pass so that he could get out.

If he had been evacuated then he was safe and all I had to do was wait for him to be allowed to come to me or to phone me. If he was in the bunker, and the fire passed over, he would eventually come to me. On the other hand if he was trapped in the bunker by fallen trees or debris then I was totally reliant on the police officer at the Whittlesea police station to pass my map onto someone else so that they could go and check the bunker.

I needed to get to the bunker at Waldene. I could not rely on the police to give priority to checking the bunker. After all, the enormous number of people at the police station and the community hall suggested there was a long list of 'priorities'. I remembered the 'back road' to the cottage. It is a long, dusty dirt road that winds around behind the Yan Yean Reservoir and eventually rolls down behind the golf course onto Humevale Road. If I drove down that road I would come out beyond the roadblock where I had earlier been turned back.

Monday 9 February 2009
Just after 1 am I drove quickly through Yarrambat towards the Yan Yean Reservoir. The roads were deserted. About 200 metres before the turn-off to the dirt road my headlights picked up a police car parked across the entry to the back road. I pulled off the road and phoned Barry's long-time friend Daniel Turnbull. Daniel and Barry had met at teachers college some 40 years ago and although they now lived a few hours drive from each other, they kept in regular contact by phone and occasional visits. Barry had introduced me to Daniel and his wife early in our relationship and I knew that they would be worrying about us. I wanted to tell Daniel what I had done so far and that I was going to try to convince the police officer to let me through the roadblock. It was 1.30 am and I did not stop to consider that Daniel may have been sleeping. It was comforting to talk through my plan with someone who knew the layout of the property and the surrounding roads.

I hung up from Daniel and drove slowly towards the police car. I parked again and got out of the car. The night was dark and eerily quiet. I felt tense. Everything depended on this next conversation. The police officer got out of his car as I approached. He was a young constable, all alone out here, blocking the back road. I had to convince him to let me through. I took a deep breath.

I told him that I needed to get to my house. I said it was just a couple of hundred metres down the road. He obviously was unfamiliar with the area or he would have known that there are no houses that close to the turn-off. He looked back down the dirt road behind him. There was no smoke or fire visible from where we stood. 'Just a couple of hundred metres?' he asked.

'Yes,' I lied. 'I just need to check that everyone's out.'

No-one was more surprised than me when he said, 'Okay, as long as it's only a couple of hundred metres in. But don't hang around if it's not safe, will you?'

I cannot recall if I thanked him. In all likelihood I did not, such was my urgency to be back in the car and driving towards the bunker and Barry. I drove the perilous few kilometres along the back road with feverish excitement. There are no street lights on the road and normally kangaroos and wallabies provide a well-known hazard. The night seemed to lay black and oppressive across the windscreen. I strained to see where I was driving and I travelled in dread of being turned back by another roadblock at any point along the road.

After what seemed an interminable time, the road dipped down and the golf course came into view on my left. I was beyond the Humevale roadblock. The plan had worked. Now all I had to do was drive down to Humevale Road and follow it uphill to Waldene.

I swung the car onto Humevale Road; past the houses, around the bend, towards the bridge. But yet again, I was forced to stop. This time a large SES truck blocked access to the bridge across Scrubby Creek. Leaving the car, I strode determinedly to where two uniformed SES men stood beside their truck. I was ready to demand that they move the truck. In the gloom I could see their soot-streaked faces above their grimy yellow overalls.

'You can't go any further,' one addressed me.

'I need to get to my partner further up the hill,' I pleaded, trying to keep the mounting hysteria from my voice. I explained about the bunker and my concern that Barry might be trapped underground.

'The pylons under the bridge are burnt. It's not safe to drive across,' one of them said.

'Well, I know the way. I'm okay to walk across the bridge and up the road to the cottage.' I tried to sound calm and rational. The SES men told me that there were fires burning in the forest beyond the bridge. I did not believe them. They pointed to the ridge behind the houses.

For the first time I noticed the glow of spot fires across the slopes. The hill was not fully visible because of the thick black smoke that hung in the air and forced its way into hair and clothes and lungs. I felt like I had stumbled into some surreal landscape. I had been so focused on getting to Waldene and driving through the darkness that I had not been conscious that much of the inky darkness was attributable to the pall of smoke permeating the night sky.

I asked the SES men if the fire had only burnt on the left hand side of the road beyond the bridge or if it had crossed the road further up. Waldene was located on the right-hand side of the road, below the ridge.

The men did not know. They said they had not been beyond the bridge. They speculated that given the nature of fire, it would most likely have burnt more fiercely on the uphill side of the road. They thought that as it had travelled from Wallan in the west it would have burnt along the ridge behind Humevale and probably stayed high up, on its way north towards Kinglake. I was reassured by their words. I asked them if I could stay in my car beside the road until morning. They would not allow this and said nothing further would happen here until daylight. They suggested that I would be better off back at Greensborough in case Barry or the evacuation centre phoned.

Reluctantly I returned to my car and drove a short distance back along the road until I turned a corner and was hidden from the view of the SES men. I pulled over to the side of the road to think. I wondered about 'bush-bashing'. Barry had often described the technique used by his bushwalking group in his younger years, where they just crashed in a straight line from one location to another without using a well-trod pathway.

I wondered about the possibility of slipping past the SES men in the dark and bush-bashing up the road until I came to Waldene. I stared out the window into the blanketing darkness broken intermittently by the glowing red pyres of burning trees and shrubs. I doubted I would be able to get past the SES men. I also doubted that I would be able to find my way in the darkness. The surreal atmosphere created by the smoke was both disconcerting and disorientating.

I wondered what Barry would expect of me. I felt small and inadequate. I mulled over what he would do if the situation was reversed. I argued with myself about the difference between Barry's experience with bush-bashing and familiarity with the hillside terrain compared with mine. I speculated on the consequences if I was caught trying to get through; I felt sure the police would not allow me near the site again.

It was almost 3 am when I drove sadly away, headed for Greensborough once again.

Four hours later, frantic and unable to sleep, I was back at the community hall in Whittlesea. A handwritten sign on a wall advised that there would be a community briefing at 9 am.

Alongside the sign someone had taped a large map of the area from Whittlesea to Kinglake. I stared hard at the map trying to establish in my mind's eye approximately where Humevale and then Waldene were located. I knew that in the crush of the crowd that would attend the 9 am briefing, I would probably be forced too far back from the map for my limited long vision to be able to identify the cottage region.

My eldest son Heath phoned me just as I entered the community hall. He wanted to know where I was. At the sound of his voice I began to cry. I explained that I had been unable to sleep and had decided that I was better off at the community hall just in case some more information became available. I was grateful that he had phoned. It comforted me to think that he was thinking of me. All my ramblings and attempts to get to Barry during the previous 24 hours had left me feeling small, ineffectual and totally alone.

Heath said he would meet me at the community hall for the 9 am briefing. I was grateful but said that I would be with the crowd rather than waiting at the door or in the car park for him. I was not prepared to miss the briefing even though I was so grateful for his support. Heath must have left his home in Diamond Creek immediately because he arrived twenty minutes before the briefing began and found me in the hall.

The briefing consisted of a man from the CFA explaining the direction of the fire and the names of some places that had been impacted. Once again I listened to details about places that I did not know, interspersed with a smattering of familiar sounding towns. I could not work out the compass directions relative to the cottage, so could not determine from which direction the fire was burning or in which direction it was travelling.

I strained to catch reference to Humevale, but none was made. I felt a mix of relief and frustration. While I wanted to hear specifically about Humevale, there was some solace in the fact that it was not mentioned as an area impacted by the fire. I felt simultaneously uncertain and yet fairly confident that Barry was somewhere, waiting to be reunited with me. Probably dirty, exhausted and angry about having to do as he was told and go through a lot of bureaucratic stuff, but safe and full of excited tales that he would retell me for years to come.

When the briefing ended Heath and I moved into the squash of people who had gathered around the CFA spokesman seeking more specific information. The briefing had apparently been too brief to satisfy everyone's needs.

Gradually the mass dispersed and I was able to ask the man if he knew anything about the hill beyond Humevale. He said that he did not have information beyond the 'big picture' information conveyed at the briefing. It seemed that he was more an analyser of terrains and wind velocity and fire speed than someone who actually fights fires from the back of a truck. He suggested that we should ask how Humevale had fared over at the Whittlesea Showgrounds where the CFA people were temporarily based.

Heath and I walked across the field to the gates of the showground. A CFA person was manning the gate to prevent entry by anyone but CFA employees. He said that he had only just started his shift and admitted that at this time he did not know any details about the fires in the local area. He suggested that we drive back up the Whittlesea-Yea Road and ask at the roadblock to Humevale where I had first been stopped the previous day.

By today, the police had moved the roadblock closer to the township, just a few hundred metres beyond the showgrounds.

This terrified me because it suggested that the fire was closer to Whittlesea than had previously been the case. I was now further away from Barry than I had been during the night. Fighting the screaming panic inside, I pulled over and began to explain my urgent need to get through to Waldene. Heath got out of his car behind me and came to add his inducements to the police officer who was blocking our way.

The officer at the roadblock chided Heath about having driven through the roadblock earlier. Heath explained that this was his first time and she suggested laughingly that there were lots of guys around now who looked like him. I was so grateful that his presence appeared to soften her attitude. She explained that the extra police roadblock was because of the increased problem of potential looters and sightseers. Heath championed my case, while I sat tear-streaked, holding my breath. Would she let us pass? Was my story worthy?

She waved us through to test our case at a roadblock further along. By 10 am we had successfully talked our way through the original police roadblock at the Humevale turn-off. The police officer at that roadblock told me that even if there was no barricade at the bridge, we were not to cross over, because there may still be some safety issues about the pylons. I promised him I would not cross the bridge, wondering at the same time how likely it was that I would keep that promise.

The thought that the roadblocks on the bridge may have been removed cheered me enormously. Surely the fire had not done much damage in this area if the roadblocks were already removed. I turned into Humevale Road and Heath followed behind in his car.

A few hundred metres further along I gestured for Heath to pull over to the side of the road. I hopped out of my car and went to tell him, almost joyfully, that there was no need for him to come any further. I knew that he had other things to do and places he should be. It was Monday 9 January 2009 and he was on his Christmas summer holidays. Heath was pleased he had been able to help. Happy that everything would be okay now, he kissed me goodbye, did a U-turn and drove back the way we had come.

I felt great excitement. At last I would be allowed to get to Barry. I drove slowly on. The spot fires on the hills behind the main street of Humevale were no longer burning. A truck came towards me along Humevale Road. This suggested that the bridge had been repaired as there are few side roads along this stretch. I had made it through. I grinned to myself, 'Very soon now, my love. What tales we'll have to tell each other.'

To my dismay, as I drove closer to the bridge I found the SES truck from the previous night had been replaced by a police car, which was parked beside the road. A police officer was leaning into a car discussing something earnestly with the driver. I parked some way back to see what was happening. The police officer straightened up and took a few steps back. The car slowly turned around and drove back the way it had come. The police officer was making people turn and go back. It seemed that even now, no-one was allowed across the bridge.

I felt a sense of rage boil up inside me. For almost 40 hours now I had been trapped like a rat in a maze, trying every which way to get to Barry. I was tired of being stopped by some, allowed passage by others, telling and retelling my tale, begging and cajoling my way centimetre by centimetre to get to Barry. I was tired of well-meaning CFA personnel and police and SES people from far-flung parts of Victoria and interstate who stopped me at roadblocks with no knowledge or news of anything. I was tired of no-one seeming to care that Barry might be buried alive underground.

I dialled Waldene's phone number on my mobile. Once again the clipped voice of the cyber phone receptionist advised me that the phone line was temporarily disconnected. I stared glumly out through the windscreen, willing the police officer to get into his car and drive away.

I considered bush-bashing again. I had never done it. Could I do it now in the daylight, I wondered? I would need to drive away and park the car secretly then double back, cross the creek somehow and find my way through the forest. The cottage was 3 kilometres by road, but it would be much further through the hills and valleys of the forest. I wondered if I would become lost.

I thought about what Barry would do if it was me trapped underground in the bunker. With shame I recognised what he certainly 'would not' do. He would not be sitting here on the side of the road obeying all the rules and waiting for permission from a police officer to go and find me. He was much better than I could ever be. He used to jokingly call me 'Miss Mouse' because I was so worried about offending or intimidating anyone.

I felt ashamed. I hoped he would understand when we finally got around to describing what happened to each of us between when we kissed goodbye on Saturday morning until the time we finally found each other again.

It is only with hindsight that I realise that there in fact was no forest left at the time I was contemplating bush-bashing to Waldene. There was a far greater chance that my shoes would have melted underfoot than that I would have become lost among the trees.

This tiny little bridge across this pathetic little waterway with the humble title of Scrubby Creek was proving to be an insurmountable hurdle. I decided to try one more plea. I drove slowly up to the police car. The police officer came over to tell me that no-one was allowed to drive any further along the road and that I should turn around. I tried to explain that I needed to get to the cottage to make sure Barry was not trapped in the bunker. The police officer remained steadfast that I would not be allowed any further along the road. I asked if I could park under a tree growing beside the road about 30 metres back from the bridge. He said that I could if I wanted too.

I parked the car. I sat for an hour watching the comings and goings of the police, the SES and the local residents. A fire truck came down the hill from the direction of the cottage. It crossed the bridge and drove past me headed for the main road. I wondered about the truth in the statement that the bridge was unsafe; if it could hold the weight of a fire truck, why not that of my small car? Perhaps soon they would open the bridge up again.

I tried to read a novel that I had brought with me. I waited and I watched.

It was a hot day. I had brought two cans of Barry's favourite soft drink with me. I was looking forward to giving them to him when we were finally reunited. He rarely drank tea or coffee and yet I knew that was probably all that would be offered at whichever evacuation centre he had been sent to. He would be delighted to see that I had thought to bring him some soft drink.

I noticed another police car parked in the front yard of the last house before the bridge. A police officer seemed to be supervising his constables conducting some sort of door-knock. I wondered what this was about; perhaps a census of who was safe and who was missing? I watched and waited. This seemed a chance to progress Barry's plight. I got out of the car and walked into the yard and stood in front of the supervising police officer. He looked up from a sheath papers that he was holding.

I explained in a tumble of words and gestures that I must get up to Waldene; that I had been trying for hours and hours, that I had driven back and forth many times along Plenty Road and Humevale Road, that I had been to the police station and the community hall, that I had filled out forms and drawn maps and left phone numbers and that there was nowhere else I could go and nothing else that I could do except remain here and wait until Barry came walking out or until someone told me that he was not able to walk out.

The police officer stood quietly while I vented my spleen. He asked me to draw a map that would show him where the bunker was located on the Waldene site. He took the map and said that he would radio to someone to see if they could at least check the site for the bunker.

I felt a rush of gratitude. At last, here was someone doing something specifically about Barry. The police officer told me to go back and wait in my car and that he would come and tell me if he found out anything about Barry. I hurried back to the car as if a prompt response to his request would gain me a prompt response to my request.

A few minutes went by. I could see the supervising police officer talking on his car radio. He was sitting in the police car with the door open. He was still holding the pile of papers in his other hand. He looked casual; like he was just making a casual enquiry to appease an overwrought woman who refused to go away until she was given something by way of information. I waited and I watched.

It was still hot. The soft drink cans would have to be cooled before Barry could open them. I wished I had brought some ice in a little esky to keep them cool. Still, I had not realised it would all take this long. At least I had brought the drinks. I fleetingly wondered if I should have brought some food for Barry as well. But no, the women's auxiliary would probably have plied him with scones and sandwiches at the evacuation centre. Barry had always liked scones. He used to buy two plain scones at the Whittlesea bakery on his way to work some mornings. I felt sure he would just be desperately in need of a soft drink after being forced to drink tea for so many hours; food would not be a problem.

Up ahead of me I saw the police officer get out of his car.

2

I leapt out of my car and hurried towards him. 'It's not good news I'm sorry,' he said. I waited, expecting that once again, nobody knew anything. The police officer looked down at the ground as if trying to remember what information he had heard on his radio.

'It seems they've found some remains at the address you gave me.' He looked up into my face. I remember wondering what he meant and I wished he would tell me what he had found out about Barry. Since then I have wondered what I was thinking about 'remains' ... possibly it registered as leftovers of the trees, the house, the forest, the garden; destroyed items; mere things. I waited.

The police officer continued. 'They were right where you described.' I felt momentarily pleased that my map had helped. I waited in silence, not wanting to interrupt him. I waited for him to tell me about Barry.

'Now we can't confirm it's Barry, but I don't want you to get your hopes up,' he said. A torrent of blood rushed through my veins and tore reason and sense from my mind. I suddenly realised what he was saying. They had found 'remains' in the bunker, just where I had described Barry would be.

I scowled at the police officer and began a trail of dialogue as I tried to make sense of the impossible. Whispering, almost to myself I rambled on, 'It couldn't be anyone but Barry. There are no visitors to Waldene. There is just Barry and me. If it's not Barry it must be a kangaroo or some animal. It must be Barry.'

I felt frantic to explain the obvious and yet with every word I hated the logic of what I was saying. It seemed to be of urgent importance to me that I explain what the reality must be. I felt that somehow I might be able to control the situation if I could just get it to make sense. It was like a very difficult jigsaw that refused to fall into place.

The police officer had become a collection of policemen when I next noticed them. I started to cry. I told them, 'It can't be right … Barry doesn't make mistakes.'

The police officer told me that I would have to go to the community hall. He said that I was to go in the police car and that a police officer would drive my car there. I replied that I would be all right to drive myself. He insisted and gently pushed me into the back seat of a police car. He no doubt realised that I was already slipping away into shock.

I hunched down in the back seat of the police car. I was conscious of mumbling over and over, 'He doesn't make mistakes. It can't be right. He doesn't make mistakes.'

I remember smiling at one point during the drive when I convinced myself that it really was a mistake. I smiled; imaging Barry finding this all very amusing when we were together again. But then, gripped again by uncertainty, I resumed my mumblings and sobbing. Like a pendulum, my mind swung back and forth trying to decide what was true and what was untrue.

In the front seat, the two police officers were speaking quietly to each other. I was not listening to them until I heard one say, 'We can't take her there. There are too many cameras.' I lost interest in them again.

Suddenly the police officer in the passenger seat barked out, 'Turn in there. There's only CFA and some Salvation Army people there.' The car swung into the Whittlesea Showgrounds, where what seemed a lifetime ago, a CFA man at the gate had told me that he had no information about the fires at Humevale.

The police car stopped and the driver got out and went inside one of the pavilions. I remained hunched in the back seat mumbling to myself. The car door suddenly opened and I was eased out of the car and into the waiting embrace of a woman. The police car drove off.

The woman guided me into a large room that was empty except for a long trestle table and two chairs. She gently pushed me down onto a chair and then seated herself opposite me. All the while she was patting my arm and murmuring comforting words, the content of which I have forgotten, but I well remember their soothing effect.

She told me that she was Major Glenys Ford, a Salvation Army officer. Much later I learnt that her intended volunteer role that day was to make tea and sandwiches for weary firefighters on their breaks. Yet here, suddenly, to shield me from the journalists surging like a school of piranha outside the community hall, the police had placed me in her care.

I continued to cry, sometimes quietly and sometimes in enormous gulping sobs that threatened to throw my heart and soul out of my body and destroy me utterly. I answered Glenys' questions incoherently, rambling backwards and forwards across my love and my life with Barry. I doubt that she made much sense of what I said, but she listened with great compassion.

It was 1.15 pm when Glenys phoned Daniel and then my girlfriend Judy, to explain what had happened. She asked Judy if she could come and collect me. Glenys also phoned Heath and asked him to organise for someone to come and get my car.

I do not know how long we sat there together. It might have been hours or days for all my mind was able to discern. No-one else came into the room; just the two of us in the barn-like surrounds.

While we waited, my phone rang. Glenys answered it and after listening to the caller she asked me if I felt up to speaking to Barry's sister. This was the first of many horrid experiences I was to endure following the fire.

Barry's sister was a very strict Christian and never forgave Barry for marrying twice and then going on to have a relationship with me when we were both technically married to other people. Even though Barry and I had been together for many years, she would not allow me into her home and often held prayer meetings to pray for Barry's repentance. Barry had written her a formal letter severing all contact with her some ten years earlier.

In my dazed state I had trouble working out who Glenys was referring to, but when I realised, I instantly recoiled. How could Barry's sister even think of phoning me now? I asked Glenys how Barry's sister had obtained my mobile phone number, given that we had never before spoken on the phone. Apparently hearing of the fires, she had contacted Daniel and he had given her my number. I was very grateful when Glenys told Barry's sister that I did not want to speak to her. My crying became even more distraught. I felt suddenly very alone and weak.

Glenys left me for a few minutes to return with a box of tissues and a large bowl of warm soapy water. She gently washed my hands. It seemed an unusual thing to do but I felt its calming effect. She whispered to someone at the door and soon I was brought a plate of thickly cut sandwiches and a mug of steaming tea. I stared at the sandwiches in awe. They seemed so huge; so perfectly right for weary firefighters. I could not bring myself to eat. Glenys insisted that I at least take a few sips of tea.

She proposed that we move our chairs outside the door for a while. The showgrounds were alive with activity. I continued to cry. The firefighters and volunteers going about their business glanced sadly in my direction as they hurried past. Realising the distress that this was causing both the firefighters and me, Glenys moved us back inside.

On we sat; just this stranger and I, alone in the cavernous hall. I felt myself sagging, folding down into my chest, shrinking. There seemed no past or future, just this present state, just here, just now; for no purpose but to breathe, to cry, to sit, to cry. I wondered if I was waiting for something. I could not be sure. I struggled to hold onto the thought. The police had said 'remains'. I wondered when Barry would come. 'Remains'; it is a plural. On we sat, me with lowered head, sobbing, floating, shrinking.

Suddenly I became aware of a shadow that filled the open doorway and Glenys quickly rose to her feet. It was my friend Judy, her hands shoved deep into the pockets of her jacket giving the impression she wore a cape. She was tall and strong and confident and she crossed the floor in huge strides to envelop me in her arms. We clung to each other, crying. Glenys stood back and waited for Judy to regain some composure.

Judy and Glenys spoke together quietly. I felt myself let go with the arrival of Judy. I no longer needed to answer questions, or listen, or think about things. Judy would look after me. She would know what to do. She was efficient and sensible and knew me better than I knew myself. A friend is a most wonderful thing.

Glenys asked if we could pray together before we separated. Neither Judy nor I are religious but there we stood, three women with their arms locked around each other. Glenys prayed that the Lord would look after us and give us the strength we needed to see our way through whatever lay ahead.

Judy put me into her car and with a final wave we left Glenys and the showgrounds to go back to Greensborough. Judy made many phone calls advising family, friends and colleagues of the situation. I sat at the kitchen table crying. I found the two teddy bears that Barry and I had had for years. Normally they lived on the bed at Waldene, but they had needed a wash and I had brought them to Greensborough the day before the fire for that purpose. I clung to the teddies. I tried to think about where Barry might be and when he might come. Everything was wrong. Even the fact that the teddies were here at Greensborough was a muddle.

Heath came with my car. My sluggish brain puzzled over how he did that. He must have gone to Whittlesea. Someone must have helped him. I felt as though I was in a fog. I did not want to talk. I wanted everything to go slow so that I might be better able to make sense of things. Perhaps if it all slowed down I would be able to find out what was wrong and work out how it could be solved. I am usually good at solving things if I can just make sense of the problem. Part of me seemed to be stuck somewhere else, accepting defeat.

Judy said I was to go to sleep. I insisted on sleeping in the bed that Barry had slept in the night before. There are only single beds in the Greensborough house. I pushed my face into Barry's pillow trying to find his scent. I curled up into the foetal position, hugging the teddies and sobbing. Judy came and lay across the foot of the bed and rubbed my back. There we lay for hours in the darkness, both of us too overwrought to sleep and unable to say anything of any consequence.

Tuesday 10 February 2009
Early next morning, I told Judy I was going back to the Whittlesea Community Hall to see if there was any news. I have no idea what value Judy saw in this. Outwardly she agreed with me and I assumed

rightly or wrongly that her assent meant that she also thought that Barry was 'alive but missing' rather than any alternative.

She said that I was in no state to drive to Whittlesea myself and that a doctor's visit was a condition to be met before she would drive me. I said that I did not need a doctor but she insisted that it might be worth having some sleeping tablets or nerve pills, given the trauma I had been through. I thought about driving myself to avoid the time needed for what I considered an 'unnecessary' doctor's visit. I could drive but I knew that my continual sobbing would be a problem once I arrived at the community hall.

The doctor prescribed some pills, which I told Judy I would not take. Judy ignored me and had the prescription filled anyway. We drove to the community hall. I felt sure that by today, Barry's name would appear on a list showing that he had finally been located; maybe in a hospital somewhere, maybe too injured to remember who he was, maybe …

As we drove towards Whittlesea my mobile phone rang. Since picking me up from Glenys, Judy had answered all my phone calls to save me having to deal with people's questions.

Judy listened to the caller for a few seconds before tears welled up in her eyes and she began shouting into the receiver, 'How can you phone her? Don't you know she's lost her partner? Where did you get this number? How can you do this? You're a scum. You've no right …' She hung up and began to cry in earnest.

When she was able to, she told me that the caller was a journalist. He had found my number on the message wall at the community hall. He wanted to know 'if Barry was still missing and if he could interview me about how I was feeling about that'.

We drove on in silence, both somewhat shocked and angry at the insensitivity of the press in their hunt to sell papers. I thought of how determined the journalist must have been that when denied entry to the community hall itself, he had milled around at the front door and craned his neck far enough to be able to read the message board in the narrow entry hall. Unbeknown to us, that morning the entire message board, including my note to Barry, appeared as a centre-page spread in the Herald Sun newspaper. At least the press had the decency to block out phone numbers from those handwritten messages of hope left by people desperately seeking their loved ones.

The Whittlesea Community Hall was crowded with people. A side room had been opened off the main hall. Judy led the way and I felt myself shrinking as I trudged along behind her. The sea of people and noise were overwhelming. Volunteers in basketball-type bibs approached us on all sides. We were gestured towards tables where toasted sandwiches and coffee were being offered for breakfast. Someone else wanted to know if we needed an immediate Centrelink hardship grant and yet another asked us about accommodation needs.

Judy waved them aside and pushed through the crowd until she found the volunteers dealing with 'missing persons'. She explained my situation. I became upset again. It was difficult to hear Barry being discussed aloud by strangers in this public place. I was conscious of the sad glances cast at me as Judy spoke.

I lowered my head so I would not have to deal with their eyes or what their glances seemed to suggest about Barry's whereabouts. Like a child, I clung to the premise that if I could not see them, they could not see me. I wanted to scream out. I wanted to tell them they were wrong; that someone had made a mistake; that they just needed to check their lists again properly and they would find Barry for me. But I felt too paralysed to even look up, let alone speak. Instead I stood there, shrunken and pathetic. Nothing was in my control anymore.

The volunteer looked through some papers, she mumbled to another volunteer who shuffled though other papers. The volunteer addressed Judy. She explained that they could not find a record of Barry having been reported as missing. Judy asked me to describe what forms I had filled in the previous day and who I had filled them in with. I described what had happened to Judy and she turned back to explain this to the volunteer.

Judy was protecting me from having to deal directly with the world, placing herself between me and any conversations with strangers. It reminded me of the protection offered by a mother to her child. I was only able to proceed because of this arrangement and I was so very grateful for Judy's presence.

No record of Barry as missing? All this time and because the paperwork was lost, no-one had been looking for him other than whoever had searched the bunker and found 'remains'. My sluggish mind tried to determine what that might mean. Was it a good thing or a bad thing? Did this bring a resurgence of hope? Could he be unconscious in a hospital or lying somewhere incapacitated and unrecognised? Surely it was possible.

Judy explained to the volunteer that I was very distraught and that she would need to be with me if we were to fill out the forms again. The volunteer took us over to a senior Red Cross volunteer. Explanations were mumbled in his ear and an extra chair appeared for Judy. The missing person form was filled out again. This time I was offered tea to soothe my sobbing, while beside me, Judy bore the brunt of the questioning.

Finally we pushed through the crowd towards the door. At the message wall I paused to remove my tiny stick-it label from its location and put it into my pocket. It seemed that by now, Barry would not need it, regardless of where he was or what had happened, and I did not want the press phoning me again.

Back at Greensborough bouquets of flowers had been delivered, sent by friends and colleagues who had heard of the situation. I was both surprised and moved by the list of people who had taken the trouble to do this. I wondered fleetingly how they had learned about it all so quickly.

I had not watched the news or listened to the radio since Saturday, and to this day am unaware of how concentrated the press coverage was. Months later, looking back at the newspapers of the time, it appears that all other news was suspended in order to cover the horrifying devastation of the Black Saturday bushfires.

Soon after our arrival at Greensborough, my eldest brother, Richard, and another long-time girlfriend, Susan, arrived, both with overnight cases and compassion. Their arrival puzzled me and brought with it a sense of foreboding. My brother was a rare visitor and never for an overnight stay. Furthermore, he never visited without his wife – and yet here he was.

Susan had occasionally stayed overnight for a 'girls' weekend' but always with much advance planning. The appearance of both of them, uninvited, was alarming somewhere inside me, yet I fell into their open arms with great gulping tears, pleased that they had come; more recruits in my hunt to make sense of all this and to find Barry.

Judy slipped away for a while and Susan took over the responsibility of answering all my phone calls. Richard sat with me for hours listening to me talk on and on about Barry and about Barry and I together. He listened as I rummaged aloud, retracing each step, each movement of the past few days. He sat quietly as I turned over every incident, every action and reaction, as I frantically searched for the missing part of the puzzle. His gentle, non-judgmental presence gave me great comfort.

I talked on and on, through the night into the milky dawn. I had only introduced Barry to Richard for the first time a couple of months earlier and if he was shocked to find that Barry and I had been living a clandestine life for over fifteen years he did not show it. Instead he listened with my father's eyes and my mother's compassion. I was his little sister once again and he would not let any harm come to me.

Meanwhile Susan assumed a role as my personal assistant. She answered phone calls, conveyed messages back and forth, filtered out problems and recorded everything that she considered important in an exercise book. She met people at the door, explained the 'situation' and gave people instructions about how long they should stay. She was not going to allow anyone through to me who she considered would be a problem and she did not care whose ego she bruised in so doing. My friends later told me that they had dubbed her the 'Gatekeeper' and they knew her as a force to be reckoned with. Her warm smile and pleasant greeting masking her firm hand on the door and on the phone receiver.

For the first few days I walked in a confused haze. I searched the Greensborough house for any relics of Barry. I put them inside my pillowcase so that I could sleep with them. I found some cards and a few letters that he had written to me, some pieces of paper where he had scribbled some words, a photo of us together, a bookmark he had given me. I began collecting 'things' and pushing them into my pillowcase. I took to carrying the bulging pillowcase around with me.

I would sit all day at the kitchen table nursing my small sack.

With hindsight I realise what a disturbing sight I must have appeared to visitors. No doubt part of Susan's mumbled conversations with people at the front door was to prepare them for the sight of me. It was to their credit that no-one ever tried to take the pillow away from me. Rather they allowed me my quiet insanity; my grip on the pillowcase as firm as my belief that Barry would soon come back.

Daniel rang and said that that he intended visiting Waldene the following day and that the police had been in contact with him to request a copy of Barry's dental records. Apparently he did not realise that it was not as easy as 'just dropping into Waldene for a visit'. Susan conveyed his conversation to me and I gave her the contact details for our dentist. She made the necessary phone call and organised that we would collect the records the next day on the way through to meet Daniel up at Waldene.

I heard the request for dental records with some degree of joy. This then would provide proof that the 'remains' were not Barry. On the other hand, if horribly the 'remains' were Barry, the fact that dental records would prove useful to identifying him indicated that his beautiful body had been found. Perhaps he had suffocated in the bunker. 'Get down low and go, go, go;' it was the chant that the CFA taught children to remember if they were ever caught in a fire. Barry and I had giggled about the double entendre sexual connotations of the chant and we had laughingly chanted it to one another on many occasions.

'Suffocation.' I wondered about it. I decided that drowning and suffocation must be similar; lack of air, struggling to breathe, coughing, gasping, unconscious – quiet, peaceful death. Barry had once said that he thought that drowning would be a good way to die, if one had to choose a method. The unconscious state that precedes the death means the person falls into a sort of sleep and therefore would not be aware that they had died; just a seamless path from sleep to death.

Fleetingly I remember being a bit jealous that the police had contacted Daniel for the dental records. Why had they not contacted me directly? Had they given him permission to visit Waldene whereas until now, access for me had been denied? Perhaps I had not pushed everyone hard enough; perhaps I should have insisted more or tried harder.

But the thoughts floated away as quickly as they had arrived. Tomorrow I was going back to Whittlesea and I was happy to conclude that I would at last be allowed to go to Waldene to search for Barry myself. After all, I knew Waldene better than anyone other than Barry. If he was there somewhere, I would find him. I would look in earnest. I would look where others may have failed to look. I would call out and he would recognise my voice. He would make a huge effort if he was injured or trapped and he would return my call. Tomorrow I would find him.

Added to this was my belief that the dental records would mean either they could identify and return Barry's suffocated body to me or we could renew our search for him in hospitals or refuge centres elsewhere, beyond Waldene. I felt sure that the latter would be the case and I slept fitfully in great anticipation of the new day and the opening of the dental clinic.

3

Wednesday 11 February 2009
Susan wanted to drive Richard and me to Whittlesea. I knew that she was unsure of how to get there and she was prone to be hysterical under stress. I wanted to drive. I wanted us to get there quickly without fuss. I could not sit beside Susan as she hesitatingly drove through traffic and roadblocks and diversions. I announced that either I would drive us or I would drive myself but I would not be driven by anyone else. Susan and Richard 'had words'. I did not care what they decided. I knew what I was going to do.

Richard read my determination. He announced that he thought I would be best to drive, justifying it by saying I knew the roads and that driving would give me something tangible to do. I was glad we did not have to argue about it, especially today when we would be allowed into Waldene and we would find Barry.

When 9 am came I was first in the door at the dentist. With downcast eyes the dentist handed over a small file. He mumbled some heartfelt sentiments about hoping that the records would help. The dentist's assistant appeared beside the dentist. She said that Mr Johnston (Barry) had been a teacher when she was a student at Mernda Primary School years earlier. She, too, wished me well.

I bounded back down the stairs and into the car. With great enthusiasm I drove towards Whittlesea.

The traffic thickened as we approached the township. It seemed that everyone was trying to get back to their homes or to check on loved ones. Police directed people along allocated roads. A new roadblock had been set up immediately outside the showgrounds. This meant that we were to be stopped even further away from Waldene than before. My heart sank. A police officer leant into the car to ask our purpose for wanting to go beyond the roadblock. I began to cry. Richard took over the task and explained in a way that reached the police officer. He directed us to turn into a road behind the showgrounds where I could apply for a wristband that would allow us to pass further roadblocks.

I parked the car and Richard asked me if I had anything to prove that I was Barry's partner. I became frantic and started mumbling about the fact that we were not married, that all the papers and documents about Waldene were in the filing cabinet at Waldene. The only document I had was the power of attorney and a photo of Barry that I had been carrying in my handbag since the fires. Until now, no-one had asked me for any form of identification.

The three of us moved onto the end of a line of people who were slowly shuffling towards two small tables at the head of the queue. Someone ahead said that they were only letting people beyond the roadblock if they could prove their house was there. I suppose with hindsight that this was to stop looters and sightseers. I felt myself shaking. I kept sobbing to Richard that I would not be allowed through because I could not prove what they wanted. I was conscious of Susan on one side of me and Richard on the other holding my arms, perhaps holding me up, I was so distraught by this time.

Richard told me to let him do the talking. He put his arm around me and said something like, 'They'll just have to look at you to know that you're genuine.' I wondered what he meant, unaware of the distressing sight that I was already presenting to the external world.

Ahead of us, a couple was being denied access beyond the

roadblock because only their business was located in the fire zone, not their house. I felt nauseous with fear and trepidation. Would I be turned away again?

It was our turn at the table. Richard explained the situation. He gestured to the plastic pocket I was holding that contained the power of attorney and Barry's photo. The woman swept a glance at me, filled out a form and proffered a red plastic wristband. Beside her, her colleague seated at the next table paused between clients and leaned over to help fasten the small strip of plastic around my wrist. I was too overcome with relief to trust myself to speak. I nodded my thanks and the tears flowed freely down my cheeks.

We hurried back to the car and once again I turned towards Waldene. In the back seat, Susan answered my mobile phone and began talking loudly and anxiously. It was Daniel. Apparently he was beyond the roadblock and waiting for us at the Humevale turn-off. I wondered how he had managed to convince the police to let him through the roadblocks.

I showed my wristband to the first roadblock and we were waved through to the Humevale Road turn-off where we encountered Daniel and his wife, Sharna. They had entered the Whittlesea-Yea Road from the Kinglake end. Entry to Humevale Road from the top was blocked off and the police had directed them to drive down to Whittlesea and try to enter Humevale Road from the other end.

Daniel spoke to Richard, advising that the police would not allow us to go further because the bridge was unsafe. When I gave Daniel the dental records he said that the police were returning to his house to collect them in the next few days. He lamented having driven such a long way and now being denied access to Waldene. He and Sharna accepted my offer to come back to the Greensborough house for a toilet stop and something to eat and drink. I was anxious to find out if he could add anything more to what I knew.

My 'norm' had become being turned away at roadblocks and I was beginning to despair of ever being allowed to go the final few kilometres to Waldene.

When tea and sandwiches had been distributed, Daniel asked me if he and I could have a private talk. The others remained indoors and Daniel and I sat on the deck that Barry had only recently built. I already loved that deck. I could 'see' Barry digging post holes and carrying enormous pine stumps over his shoulder. At each step in the process he had called me over to explain what he was doing and why. He seemed to be good at everything he turned his hand to. Little did I realise how many of these impromptu lessons would come back to help me when I set out alone to rebuild some of the original structures at Waldene. So there we sat; Daniel appearing calm and in control, me a vague, distressed shell of a woman trying to make sense of the nonsensical. He asked me if I would be rebuilding Waldene or would I take the insurance money. I was startled; surely Waldene must be rebuilt. I stared at him dumbfounded.

'Why are you asking me?' I mumbled, unsure if I meant about the money or rebuild, or because he was ignoring that there was no confirmation of Barry's death yet, or because I was in no state for this conversation. I wished Richard and Susan were here to speak for me.

'Well, you're the sole beneficiary,' Daniel replied. I had not even thought about Barry's will. I just wanted him back. I felt a wave of something akin to anger coming from Daniel. I waited, unsure what was behind his attitude.

Daniel said that he was the executor of the will and that Barry had left instructions that there was to be no funeral service and that his remains were to be cremated and scattered. My world caved in at these words. In great anguish I begged Daniel to ignore those instructions and to give the 'remains' to me to bury or cremate, inter or scatter as I felt appropriate.

Daniel said that he was the executor of the will and as such he was obliged to follow Barry's wishes and have his remains cremated and scattered.

I began to cry. I begged him over and over. I said that if Barry had written that in his will, he would have been thinking that if he died before me, I would have the whole of Waldene and all of its belongings to remember him by. I would have all the books and letters we had shared, the bed we had slept in, the fireplace we had sat in front of, the garden that we had wandered. Barry would never have been so cruel as to leave me with nothing to remember him by.

However, it seemed that Daniel would not budge. The ashes were to be scattered.

In an effort to appease me, Daniel suggested that perhaps he could buy me 'a beautiful silver chain and locket and we could put some of Barry's ashes in the locket for me to wear around my neck'.

I was horrified at the thought of Barry's remains being separated into two portions. I could not get beyond a vision of Barry's index finger in a locket while his body floated as ash above the mountains and creeks. It was too awful, like a retelling of Solomon's child.

At that moment I knew that I would fight for Barry's ashes. I felt sure that if Barry could have foreseen the circumstances surrounding his death, he would have expected Daniel as the executor to make some concessions on my behalf. I was not above fighting, stealing or whatever it would take. But if Barry's ashes were all that was left, I would have them or die in their quest.

Not conscious of the horror I was feeling, Daniel continued

speaking, telling me that while Barry's instructions precluded a funeral service, Daniel had already contacted Trades Hall about holding a memorial service there for Barry. He spoke about the need for a public ceremony where people could honour Barry's life. I was grateful that Daniel had thought to do this. Barry was a long-time trade unionist and would have been very proud to know he had been farewelled at Trades Hall. My joy at the thought of a Trades Hall service was accompanied by my continued pleading to be allowed to have his ashes.

Daniel kept speaking. Barry had left strict instructions that his sister was not to be contacted or involved in anything to do with what happened to him after his death. At this point I spoke of my distress at receiving her phone call after Daniel had given her my mobile number. I found this puzzling now that Daniel had told me about Barry's instructions to preclude his sister from anything relating to his death.

Perhaps as a result of misinterpreting my confusion, Daniel suggested that Barry's sister could be invited to the memorial service if I wanted her to come. I roused enough to say that if Barry did not want his sister invited then she should not be invited. It seemed that the degree to which Daniel was prepared to adhere to different aspects of Barry's instructions was entirely arbitrary. Yet he would not allow me to have the ashes.

Standing up, Daniel signified that our private chat had come to an end. Back in the house he said he would be in contact with me. He shook hands and thanked Susan and Richard and then ushered Sharna out through the front door and they drove away.

I collapsed into a chair and related the sorry tale of what had transpired to Richard and Susan. It seemed to me that Daniel had asked to speak to me privately so that he would not have to defend his decisions to anyone but me. He must have known that I would be in no state to take action to change his mind.

I sobbed loudly. I could not get beyond the fact that I was to be denied all that remained of my darling Barry. There was no longer a cottage in the forest, no furniture with which to reminisce bygone days, no photos or letters to show we were a pair, no clothing that I could wear to feel forever his height, his breadth, his body odour, no voice, no face, no garden, no love. All that remained was whatever the police had labelled 'remains'. I felt like I had run up every road, asked every person, pursued every possibility, filled out every form, and all to no avail. Barry was now something called 'remains' and now it appeared that they too, would be taken from me.

Daniel had said that I was the sole beneficiary. All I wanted was for Barry to be returned to me. How could I be denied that? I could not hold my grief, my anger, my frustration. I begged my brother to do something. Barry would never have wanted me to be this upset. He had never hurt me while he was alive and I was very sure that he would not have expected Daniel would behave in this way towards me after he had gone. I thought the only reason Barry would have appointed Daniel as the executor of the will would have been to save me any worry about all the red tape. Barry could never have foreseen this outcome.

Richard sat beside me and allowed me to vent my frustration and anguish. He said that he would phone Daniel and discuss the matter. Throughout our conversation I was conscious of being thrown back to my childhood. As a little girl, Richard had always been my idol. My mother said that it was Richard who had named me Suzanne and that as a four-year-old, presented with his own sister for the first time, he had become instantly enchanted.

'My big brother'; in my eyes he was taller and stronger and

more handsome than all the other boys at school. In my eyes there was nothing he could not achieve. He played sport, was academic, charmed teachers and girls alike. His manners in other people's homes had him held up as an example by other mothers to their sons. He did not openly acknowledge me in the school yard, in fact, he told me to stay away from him if I insisted on eating liquorice bars that left black smudges on my face and a black ring around my mouth. But I never doubted that he was always there for me if I needed him.

Decades earlier, when in primary school, a boy in my class had made sport of yanking my plaits until I screamed. I tried everything to dissuade him from doing this, all to no avail. After several days, Richard had found me hiding in my room, hunched over my knees sobbing. After hearing my tale and learning the culprit's name he told me not to worry about it anymore; he would 'fix it'. Richard intercepted the boy walking home from school and my plaits were never pulled again. Some weeks later Richard took me around to a neighbour's fence to point out the chipped brick where the boy had hit his head during their fight.

And now … here I was some 50 years later relying on my big brother to save me again. I did not doubt for a minute that he could do it. When he told me that he would 'speak to Daniel' I knew Richard would get me Barry's 'remains'.

Richard waited until the evening to give Daniel enough time to drive back to the country town where he and Sharna lived. Then leaving me still clutching my pillow of 'treasures' in the kitchen, he went into another room to make the phone call. I strained to hear what was said. Richard's soft phone voice meant that only fragments carried the distance. I heard him say, 'But you don't understand. To her, the ashes are Barry. She couldn't wear some in a necklace. That would be like cutting Barry into pieces.'

I sat – waiting yet again. I was unaware back then that many of the years stretching before me would be spent waiting; waiting for information, for statements to be taken, for bureaucratic decisions to be made, for new legislation to be drafted, for the receipt of necessary paperwork, for permission to be given, for objections to be lodged, for applicable approvals, for regrettable rejections, for slow commencements and for even slower completions. Life alone, beyond Black Saturday, keeps its own time. It knows nothing of clocks or calendars or just or unjust. It tests those waiting to the extreme, hoping that at some point they might surrender. Some people did wander off, down to where their paddocks and yesterdays used to be. Their waiting was too great. They had to give up.

I heard Richard hang up. He sighed and remained for a moment or two beside the phone. I waited. Only now can I realise the enormity of the task that lay before him. He must have stood there, alone and devastated, turning over what he had to tell me. Richard came to sit beside me. He said that as the executor, Daniel wanted to carry out Barry's wishes but that he was willing to compromise. He said that Barry's ashes did not perhaps need to be scattered at Mount Feathertop or even Scrubby Creek as per Barry's wishes. Daniel must have reckoned that I was in fact unlikely to rebuild Waldene, hence scattering the ashes in Scrubby Creek, which borders the property, might be redundant.

I looked at Richard, waiting for the compromise. Richard put his arm around me and said quietly, 'Is there somewhere that Barry liked to be; some place special? We might be able to scatter the ashes there instead.'

I turned my face fully to look at him. I wondered that he could not see the obvious. 'He likes to be with me,' I said. 'He would want to be with me.'

At this, Richard let out a deep, involuntary sob. He struggled to drag a handkerchief from his pocket and then wept quietly beside me. I sat and waited, tears welling up in my eyes. It seemed that this time my big brother may not be able to help me.

'I'm sorry,' he mumbled into his handkerchief. 'You just brought me undone for a minute.'

There we sat; side by side, tear-stained and tired, trying to think our way through a nightmare. Another restless night, made worse for me by the knowledge that Richard was going home the next day. He wanted to research other avenues that we might try, in order to secure Barry's ashes. We had been raised in a family that believed in honesty and fairness and kindness. Along with that we had learned that the government and the legal system protect the innocent and we felt sure that somehow Daniel could be prevented from scattering Barry's ashes.

4

Thursday 12 February 2009
Richard left early, promising he would be back and that in the meantime he would be trying to find out what legal powers Daniel had as executor. It was with great sadness that I watched him leave. He had given me someone to lean upon and to stand behind for protection when the going got too difficult. The fact that he was doing this for me, in spite of the fact that he had only met Barry a few times since we had made our relationship public, cemented my admiration for him. True to our family lore, when told that I was in trouble, he had arrived, and without question taken his place alongside me.

Soon after, Judy arrived and Susan drove the three of us once again towards Waldene. Finally today, four days after the fires had raced across the hills, the police at each roadblock waved us through. Closer and closer we got. I held my breath as we approached the Humevale turn-off where we had met Daniel and Sharna. The police officer leant into the car. I showed him my wristband. He said that the bridge was still out but suggested we try driving down from the top end up at Coombs Road. I wondered if there would be more roadblocks at the top end but I did not bother to ask him. I was ready to drive to Waldene via Darwin if there was a chance of getting to the site.

The silence in the car as we drove the 6 or 7 kilometres of winding road towards Coombs Road was deafening. Our car was a tiny smudge of blue on a blackened canvas. The skeletal remains of the forest were bent and twisted; the raised tree limbs seemingly trapped in their upward appeal to Heaven for mercy. Nothing moved, no sound, no colour, no life. Here and there, sheets of curled iron appeared flung around collections of rubble; a suggestion of some previous shelter. A burnt-out car sat twisted and hunched on the shoulder of the road. The red and white stripe of the police crime tape stretched across its charred remains acted as protective arms, attempting to shield its horror from the public gaze. The tape hinted for passers-by to look ahead and drive past respectfully.

On and on we drove. The white line down the centre of the road had perished in the fire. The road and the landscape were unrecognisable. I found it difficult to orientate myself. I was relieved when we came to the concrete roadside tanks that mark the turn into Coombs Road. Humevale Road snaked away down to our right. I sent up a silent prayer of thanks as Susan turned the car into Humevale Road and we began the slow descent towards the cottage.

We travelled in silence, our combined sense of shock at what we were driving through hanging palpable in the air between us. The verdant undergrowth that had once jostled for space beside the road, plant tumbling upon plant, reflecting the sun and dancing with the breeze, was all gone. Like a beautiful young virgin subjected to a most horrifying and vile rape, Humevale Road now appeared naked, painfully thin, and silent. Susan drove slowly around the bends, at times having difficulty determining the division between the black tar of the road and the black powder that had become the forest floor.

Suddenly the steep driveway to Waldene appeared on our left. Instead of the pretty cottage in the forest that had always conjured up memories of fairy tales, the driveway led down to a landscape in chaos. Twisted and tortured sheets of roofing iron, charred wood and debris had been flung all around as if in a frenzy.

From the road we could see the white cast iron table and chair setting where the secret garden used to be. Years earlier after watching the movie *The Secret Garden*, Barry had dug out and paved a tiny terraced area between the house and my writing studio. It was to be my very own secret garden. He planted clumps of dahlia bulbs on either side of the paved area and a collection of canna lilies across the front. The whole area was enclosed inside its own wire fence, with access gained through a gate on the fourth side. Barry had bought a white cast iron table and chairs set and we would often sit there above the valley, hidden from view behind the trees. In summer our tea parties took place amidst a riot of flaming red dahlias and sunshine yellow lilies.

There was no trace of the garden save the cast iron setting and some of the paving. The table remained upright, but the chairs were both thrown on their backs as if the people at a tea party had been interrupted and left in great haste, upturning their chairs as they rushed away. The garden setting seemed incongruous; white bleached bones against the black landscape.

We parked at the top of the driveway and began the walk down towards the devastation. The stone chimney that Barry had built was still standing. It had lost many of the stones and the mortar had started to crumble, but it held on, proud and upright, waiting for someone to come: the elder statesman holding the fort all alone until help arrived.

Underfoot were lumps of melted glass and indefinable remnants of items that only a few days earlier had stood orderly on shelves or neatly inside cupboards.

The iron roof of the bunker had been ripped off and thrown to one side. Enormous tyre tracks criss-crossing the area indicated where the police and SES vehicles had been. They had torn the bunker apart and backfilled the cavity where Barry had sought refuge underground. The bunker now appeared as a shallow hollow in the side of the hill. I struggled across the soft soil to where Barry must have been found. I realised that had the police not backfilled the bunker I would have tried to climb in. I needed to be sure that Barry was not still there somewhere, somehow overlooked by the police and the rescue team. I began to cry. Judy and Susan urged me to come up and look through the debris that once was the cottage.

I climbed back up from the bunker and followed them into the mayhem. Susan winced, saying she could feel the ground was still hot in some places through the thin soles of her shoes. We spent a few hours lifting sheets of twisted metal, searching for trinkets. Daniel had sent instructions that we must find the safe and remove its contents. I found the safe by orientating myself between the chimney and a concrete set of steps that had also managed to survive to some degree. Under a pile of rubble the safe lay bloated and buckled. It had been squashed as the walls of the upstairs bedroom had tumbled down onto it. The door of the safe hung loosely, exposing a small collection of powdered ash inside. Anything that it had protected had perished without trace.

I located the filing cabinet in which Barry had stored all the love letters we had sent back and forth to each other throughout our eighteen years together. Even when he had written letters to me he had always made a copy of his letter before he posted it. His collection had always been complete, organised and beautiful. On occasions we had lain beside each other in bed and read collections of the letters aloud to each other. It was a most wonderful experience to hear Barry actually 'say' the words he had written to me rather than reading them myself when they arrived by post.

The filing cabinet had also taken the full impact of the upstairs collapse during the fire. It lay on its side half-buried in the earth. The buckled drawers remained locked. The metal had torn open along various seams of the drawers and with help from Susan and Judy I was able to lever open each one. The 'reward' for our effort was huge puffs of white powdered ash that floated out into the air as I pushed around the inside of the drawers with a stick. One drawer offered a few partial sheets of blackened paper with some typed text vaguely visible. My heart leapt. Perhaps this was one of his letters. Perhaps it would contain some sort of message for me. Standing up I stared hard at the two scraps of charred paper trying to make sense of the typed print.

They were pages from a poetry book. Again, my heart leapt. In the insanity that was already drawing me in, I felt sure that finding poetry amidst all this bedlam was surely some sort of sign that Barry was alive somewhere. It would be too cruel not to reunite these two hearts in love.

I still have the blackened pages of poetry. I mounted them on black satin in a small black photo frame. They are not the sort of poetry I had hoped for. One is coarse and old fashioned. It is not a poem for which Barry would have even chosen the book. The text that is readable says:

From De rerum natura, Book IV
Of like importance is the posture too
In which the genial feat of love we do;
For of the females of the four-foot kind
Receive the leapings of their males behind
So the good wives, with loins uplifted high
And leaning on their hands the fruitful stroke may try;
For in that posture will they best conceive
Not when supinely laid they frisk and heave.

For active motions only break the blow
And more of strumpets than of wives they show
When [... illegible and burnt ...] the mingled liquors flow
Endearments [... illegible and burnt ...] and too brisk a bound
Throws down the plough-share from the furrowed ground.
But common harlots in conjunction heave;
Because 'tis less their business to conceive
[... illegible and burnt ...] delight and to provoke the deed
A trick which honest wives but little need
Nor is it from the gods or Cupid's dart
That many a homely woman takes the heart
[... illegible and burnt ...] wives well-humoured, dutiful and chaste
[... illegible and burnt ...] will hold their wandering husbands fast
[... illegible and burnt ...] the links of love and such love will last.

The other poetry fragment offers more of a message. I read it often, because it survived when all our loves letters perished. I examine each word. I say it softly, slowly; trying to glean something buried deep inside the poem. It rhymes poorly and has an ungainly rhythm. When spoken aloud it stumbles and stops, then rushes along. There seems to be some solace in the words, but I cannot yet explain what they mean about Barry and me. The title is missing. It reads as follows:

Now let us sport us while we may
And now like amorous birds of prey
Rather at once our time devour,
Than languish in his slow chapped power.
Let us roll all our strength, and all
Our sweetness up into one ball
And tear our pleasures with rough strife
Through the iron gates of life.

LOST

This though we cannot make our sun
Stand still, yet we will make him run.
> – Andrew Marvell (1623–78)

Some four years after Black Saturday my grief counsellor asked me to tell her about my first visit to Waldene after the fires. Our conversation elicited a description of a photo of me that I keep recalling. It is primarily a photo of the devastation at Waldene taken by Susan on that first day that we were allowed entry. I am partly visible in the photo, just by virtue of chance. I am bent over, searching among the already rusting, twisted sheets of roofing iron, surrounded by a sea of debris that once was the kitchen.

I wrote the following passage for the grief counsellor, to explain what I was thinking:

> *I repeatedly see this photo in my mind's eye and I ponder. The 'girl' in the photo is wearing sort of little-girl, buckle-up, lightweight shoes. Her hair is shiny and she looks reasonably clean and orderly. I can almost see her; treading gently over the debris, gingerly lifting a sheet of iron here, studying a lump of molten glass there. She is searching for 'things' – tiny mementos of the house, of Barry, of their time together. She is still not convinced that there has not been some terrible mistake. She feels … 'afloat'.*
>
> *She is doing what she can, what is expected, but she anticipates that Barry will arrive anytime soon; grinning, grimy and SAFE. In the meantime she is happy enough to start foraging for artefacts on his behalf. She looks for large, obvious items, rejecting the broken bits of crockery, charred and bent cutlery, the twisted bicycle and old rabbit traps handed down to Barry from his father.*

Time passes. She stands and stares into the distance remembering the line from the Dylan Thomas play that Barry took her to see. 'Listen. Listen ... to time passing.' Still Barry does not arrive. She begins to scour the site for tarnished door handles and fallen hinges. She unearths an ugly vase, fully intact, and some fragments from the fairy statues that used to sit atop the little bed in the 'white room'. She delights at finding the blade from the circular saw that he used when he first built Waldene. She uncovers a buckled old kerosene lantern that they had used when they pitched a tent in the lounge room and practised 'camping' in anticipation of her first bushwalk over a decade ago.

She assembles her 'rag-tag' collection, touching each piece lovingly. She packs it up carefully and takes it away for safekeeping. She fails to recognise how pathetic the objects would appear to any 'would-be' thief.

Some weeks or months later the Grocon clean-up team arrives to clear the site. She wants this to happen. She cannot rebuild while the twisted iron, exploded gas tanks and unrecognisable molten mounds remain on the site. She sits in her car, parked on the roadside watching all day, as the team drives their machinery around crushing and stacking and removing.

When they finish and the large trucks and all the machinery leave, she comes to see what has been achieved. She is appalled. It is as if the precious memory has been 'skinned alive'. She feels almost physical pain as she walks alone across the naked ground, scarred with the tracks of the last machine to withdraw from the 'rape' – nothing ... nothing ... nothing.

Relentlessly she scans the ground. Now she seizes on even small pieces of broken crockery, a bent fork, a nail, a small glob of golden glass. She feels her world shrinking. On hands and knees she crawls slowly across the scraped earth; searching, searching. Having the site cleared was a terrible mistake, she realises now. Perhaps she has made many mistakes. She wonders if it is possible that Barry won't be coming back. Yet at the same time she fears what he will think when he sees what she let them do to Waldene.

You asked me what I would say if I could speak to the 'girl' in the photo. I thought about it. It's so very sad. I know her story. I know how it ends. I feel so sorry for that girl with the lightweight, little-girl, buckle-up shoes. She does not foresee the enormous weight that is about to fall upon her shoulders and the darkness that will descend across her whole existence.

Soon everything will be different for her. Everything that was light and funny and loving and joyful will disappear. Instead she will be surrounded by 'issues' and everything private will be held up to the light and made public. Everything that was beautiful will be tarnished and she will be made to feel ashamed. Friends will become strangers and strangers will become friends. Like Alice in Wonderland she will have to go deep down inside herself and stay small in order to survive. She will have to walk alone because no-one else will understand or know or remember or eventually even care. She will have to source the thing inside that was the beginning and made it matter – once found, that 'thing' will be her strength and her courage and it will see her through. She will walk on, but neither the path nor the destination will necessarily be apparent. She will only know what is the wrong way, rather than which direction she should take or why.

If I was alongside her in the photo, I would use all my strength to lift up all the tin and debris and I would tell her to search high and low for mementos. I would tell her to go slow and to pick up every broken cup and every rusting spoon, the *bicycle frame, all the coloured glass – to collect it all – because that is all that will ever remain of the physical sense of Barry, and of Barry and her together.*

I would tell her that Barry probably was not going to come back; that instead she would have to wait to go to him. I would say that she would need to be the keeper of the story if it was to be told; that there was a great deal to be done before she could go to Barry and that she just may need all those mementos to help her through the bad times ahead and to remind her that is was, and what it was and what it meant.

I would not tell her of the endless bureaucracy she would have to navigate, of the friends she would lose on the journey or of the strangers who would help to hold her up when she stumbled. I would not tell her of all the tears she would cry or the courage she would have to find. I would not tell her to swap her silly little-girl, buckle-up shoes for work boots. I would not tell her that she would need to almost become a 'man' to survive what lies ahead and I would not tell her how old she would be in just a few short years. I would not tell her that no matter how hard she worked or how fast she worked, there would always be more left to do than what she had done, at the close of every day. I would not tell her how quickly the pages would fall from the calendar without Barry to create spaces between the days of her life.

Instead I would just encourage her to keep sifting through the rubble. Tomorrow is time enough for her to learn that her past life is over and that the most that she can hope for now is to fight for a space where she will always be able to hear its echo.

Susan, Judy and I spent a few hours at Waldene that first day. We tried then abandoned our attempts at moving some of the heavy metal and rubble, opting instead to burrow underneath searching for any items that may have survived.

In the mess that marked all that remained of my small writing studio, I could find nothing familiar. Sobbing, I found myself gathering the large globs of glass that indicated where the windows had exploded and melted, returning to liquid glass before resetting in pools when the fire has passed through. I made a small cairn of glass chunks. There seemed nothing else to be done at the time.

We gathered up the small collection of items found. Judy and Susan walked back to the car. I stood for a while beside the bunker. I was reminded of the time that Barry and I had sat beside my mother's hospital bed after she had passed away – a fragment of suspended time; where one wished they could just remain; still and quiet forever. Standing there beside the bunker I wished that I could do that; just stand there and wait.

Susan and Judy called to me. Dragged back to the horror of the here and now, I turned and walked back to the car. On our return to Greensborough, Judy left to attend her mother's birthday celebration. This must have been a difficult switch in emotions for Judy.

Later that evening the *Herald Sun* newspaper phoned. Susan answered it and after listening to the caller, suggested I should take the call. It was someone working in the memorial column section of the newspaper. As Barry's next of kin, the newspaper wanted to print a free memorial notice from me in the next day's issue. They offered a generous letter count and advised me that legally they were unable to print anyone else's notices for Barry until my notice appeared in print in one of the daily papers.

I became confused. I wanted other people to be able to put in a notice if they wanted to, but I could not think of what words I might say that would be worthy of Barry. Vaguely I held onto the notion that Barry might eventually get to read whatever I wrote and I wanted him to be proud of what I had written. I tried to explain all this to the caller. The voice at the other end of the line listened patiently. She said perhaps it was too rushed to give her any text right now. She said that I should think about what I wanted written and that I could call her back any time until 9 pm. If I phoned after 9 pm, however, it would be too late for tomorrow's deadline.

I hung up the phone. I tried hard to think of some words. I have written teacher reference books, training programs, articles for various newspapers and education journals. I usually find it easy to write and yet now I could not find any words. I became upset. With hindsight, the fact that I did not yet believe that Barry was gone was a major hindrance to me being able to write his memorial piece. Susan suggested I think about some of the sentiments I had written in cards and letters to Barry.

I remembered a drawing Barry had done for me after I had visited his classroom once. I had commented on a large sketch of an Easter rabbit that he had drawn on the blackboard and I had chided Barry for never drawing pictures for me. He had asked me what I wanted him to draw for me and I had answered, 'Anything … draw me anything, even a box would be nice. Just draw me something.'

I received his drawing some days later. He had posted it to my work address. It was a pencil sketch of a room inside a castle. The room is lit by tall candelabras and features two star-filled windows. Occupying most of the centre of the room is a huge locked crystal box containing a pretty, four-poster bed, complete with ornate canopy. The bed is adorned with red-love hearts, diamonds and yellow flowers. The crystal box bears the label *'The home of my beautiful, beautiful princess*'. The whole sketch is carefully coloured in soft pencil colours of blue and pink and yellow. In one corner Barry had written, 'You said, "Draw me a box"! Will this do? I love you.'

Across the bottom of the sketch Barry had written a poignant phrase about what love means. It was this phrase that now reflected what I needed to say in his memorial notice. I had shown Susan and Richard the sketch at some time since the fires. I had cried as I tried to explain what it all meant. I looked in my pillowcase. The sketch was not there. I called to Susan for help to find the treasured piece of paper. We searched frantically. The time was ticking on and I was becoming hysterical. I sobbed that it was all too hard. I could not do it. I begged Susan to phone the newspaper and just tell them to forget it; that it was too much to ask of me.

Susan calmed me and we sat down to think. She suggested that I did not need to find the sketch at the moment, but just remember the phrase that Barry had written. I insisted that I needed to find the sketch. Susan promised we would keep looking but that I should just try to remember the phrase. I tried. Everything seemed a jumble. I was overwrought. I wrote some of the words down, scribbled them out, and began again.

Susan left me alone to think my way through the task. I felt a rising sense of panic. How could I have forgotten the words already? What did this mean? What if I forgot everything? What if I forgot Barry? I tried again and again to revive the phrase. I finally decided that I had it and yet somehow I felt that it was still slightly incorrect, even though the sentiment was right.

I showed Susan. She thought it was what she remembered reading when I had shown her the original sketch. She said that if I was happy with the phrase I had written she could still phone it through to the newspaper in time for the deadline. I wrote the introductory text that was from my heart to Barry's. This required no memory searching; the words came like the beginning of a fairy story – soft, gentle and somehow familiar. Susan took my scribblings and phoned the newspaper.

Later that night, Susan found the sketch. It was propped up on the mantelpiece. I must have put it there after showing it to Richard and Susan. Somehow I had failed to return it to my pillowcase for safekeeping. The phrase I had written was similar but slightly different to what Barry had written but close enough that I was not stressed by the difference.

Susan and I went to bed. It was six days since the fire and today I had finally been allowed into Waldene, but although I had searched and searched I had not been able to find Barry. I slept fitfully, trying hard to think where else he might be.

The next day the memorial column contained this notice:

JOHNSTON, Barry
A humble 'librarian' and a 'princess' – a love story
that will forever whisper through the forest.
Sleep softly, my love
until awakened by my kiss.
Love places in bondage those who are free and gives freedom
to those in bondage.
– Sue

5

Friday 13 February 2009

I woke early, worrying that someone would steal the secret garden setting from Waldene. I fretted about how I could get it brought to Greensborough for safekeeping. It was very heavy and I knew it would not fit in my car.

I wanted to go back to Waldene to check that it was still there. Susan tried to calm me. Another girlfriend, Katie, was flying down from Sydney to be with me. We were to pick her up at the airport this morning.

The phone rang incessantly at Greensborough. Susan answered all the calls. I just sat waiting, holding my pillowcase of treasures. I hardly ate or spoke. I tried to think my way through, to work out what I must have overlooked in my search for Barry.

Daniel rang to ask if we had located the safe. Judy rang and said she would organise for her partner to drive me up to Waldene in his small truck on Sunday. She promised that he would be able to collect the garden setting and bring it back. Major Glenys Ford from the Salvation Army phoned and Susan put me on the phone. I cried and rambled on for a few minutes. Glenys said that she would send me a diary to write in and some brochures to read that might help me deal with the grief.

My memory is that I sat at the end of the kitchen table for years. Hunched over my pillowcase, the sun streaming in the window onto my back, I was only vaguely aware of what was going on around me. I longed to just go wherever Barry was. People asked me questions and I answered. I was told to go to bed, to drink tea, to speak on the phone, to try to remember facts and details. It was a blur that carried on automatically, somewhere beyond the fringes of my caring.

An army of people came and went; people I knew, people I had never met, police, social workers, friends of Barry's, friends of mine, relations, neighbours. At the same time other people phoned. Sometimes Susan would put me on the phone to speak, sometimes I would hear her murmuring to whoever had rung that I was not really 'up to' talking at the moment.

Gradually the dining room table became buried beneath a covering of wreaths and floral bouquets brought by a fleet of delivery vehicles or left unannounced at the front door. They bore cards that expressed sorrow for my loss, wished me courage, offered me love or spoke of the sender's high regard for Barry. I stared at the flowers. Surely these wellwishers were leaping to the wrong conclusion. Barry had not been identified by the Coroner yet. He might still be alive. He could still be injured, unconscious, disorientated, suffering amnesia. Why was everyone so willing to consider him 'perished'? They did not know Barry as well as I did. Barry did not make mistakes. Something would turn up. *Faith – have faith*, I told myself as I waited.

I remember my eldest son Heath called in a few times. I was aware of him standing forlornly in the kitchen, casting worried glances in my direction and happy to do whatever Susan ordered him to do. I have his handwriting in the book that was kept beside the phone. He obviously assumed the role of receptionist for some of his visits. Another time I remember he arrived with his partner Helena and their three-month-old baby, Mia, my first grandchild. They handed Mia to me hoping that her presence would bring me back. I looked down at the baby vacantly. Heath bent down and murmured to me, 'She needs you, Grandma.'

Holding back a flood of tears, I looked up at him. 'No she doesn't,' I said softly. 'She has you and Helena.' My words must have hurt him. He had never seen me so distraught, and he was hoping that bringing Mia would alleviate my grief. I was in no condition to explain to him how alone and confused I was feeling.

Daniel phoned to say that he had organised for a memorial service for Barry to be held at Trades Hall on 25 February. He too, appeared to have given up hope that Barry was alive.

Daniel said he would suggest that everyone could go to the John Curtin Hotel opposite Trades Hall after the service. He said that way the visitors could buy their own drinks and we would not need to cater food. I was appalled at this.

I said that if old people came to the service they would be expecting at least a cup of tea and a biscuit. Daniel argued with me. I said that I could not have Barry's guests treated like that and that I would pay for the catering. In the end Daniel agreed to investigate what was possible.

Although Daniel had made the booking at Trades Hall, I was fairly confident that it would all be unnecessary anyway. The date set was almost a fortnight away. Anything could happen by then, even Barry returning, I told myself in secret. I was slowly realising that voicing my beliefs out loud caused everyone around me distress. I was apparently alone in my optimism that Barry would be found.

Detective Senior Constable Fernando Cartagena phoned and made an appointment to come to the house and interview me on Monday 16 February. He said he would bring another police officer and a counsellor along with him. He said that all next of kin to persons missing since the fires were being interviewed. The police needed to collect certain information about Barry that could be matched against data that came in from various sources.

Barry's friend Steve phoned to ask if he could visit me. He arrived bringing his wife and two young children with him. I saw a look of shock cross his face when he saw me at the kitchen table holding my pillowcase. I had not eaten for days and was feeling somewhat dazed and tired. I just wanted someone to tell me that this was all a mistake and that Barry had been found. I no longer cared what people thought. I avoided staring into their faces, preferring to talk quietly from some vantage point deep inside myself, shielded from the doubting eyes of those who had given up hope.

Steve wanted to know everything that had happened. His children sat at the table working on some colouring books while I retold the story. The absurdity of those children bent over their colouring as my horror unfolded around them still lingers in my mind. Fleetingly I wondered why Steve had brought them to hear such a tale, but the thought left me as easily as it had arrived. Rather, I just droned on, telling one fact after another, lining the details up like the pages in a diary. I knew every detail. I had repeated the tale over and over each time I had been asked on the phone or in person.

Steve reminisced about how much he had enjoyed the annual pool room competition that Barry had hosted at Waldene some years earlier. I remembered the last time Barry had held the competition. The small number of guests had meant that I was forced to play to make up the teams. It had been a fairly one-sided competition, given I had never played before. I was grateful to talk to Steve about Barry and the fun we had all shared. It brought Barry from the past into the present, keeping him alive in our conversation at least.

Saturday 14 February 2009

It was Valentine's Day. Susan, Katie and I got up early and I drove us up to the Coombs Road end of Humevale Road. I had bought some yellow carnations from the little market stall in Bundoora where Barry used to buy me two bunches of carnations each fortnight. As I bought the flowers I wanted to explain to the stallholder who I was, and why I needed the flowers. I could not get the words out. Just thinking of what I wanted to say brought tears to my eyes. I paid for the flowers and hurried back to the car.

About 20 metres along Humevale Road I was forced to stop. A newly erected temporary barricade had been placed across the road since we had been here on Thursday. A sign on the barricade advised that the road was closed. I began to cry. It seemed that I would never again be given free access to Waldene. Some cruel power seemed hell-bent on teasing me with possibilities and then clawing them back just when they appeared within my grasp.

We sat there, parked at the barricade; three middle-aged women obeying the rules. We got out of the car and walked to the barricade. It was portable. We stared down beyond it. The road curved towards a bend before disappearing in search of Waldene some kilometres away. Susan suggested we try to squeeze the car through the gap between the edge of the road and the barricade. We discussed the legality of ignoring the 'road closed' sign. Perhaps the road had collapsed somewhere further down.

Katie suggested we move the barricade and just drive slowly down to Waldene and suffer the consequences if we were later seen as law-breakers. I was grateful for their willingness to break the law in order to get me to Waldene. We paced around in the sunshine for a few moments trying to make a decision.

Unexpectedly a ute pulled up beside us. A man hopped out and called out gaily, 'Make sure you don't dehydrate, ladies!' as he handed us a slab of bottled water. Apparently he had come up with the idea of helping by driving around the back roads in the area to do this. We explained why we were standing in the middle of the road. He said that he was an off-duty police officer and that it would be all right for us to move the barricade and drive through to Waldene. He said the barricade had been installed to discourage looters and sightseers. It seemed horrible to think that looters and sightseers were even active in the area.

We quickly did as the police officer suggested and I was soon once again at Waldene. Katie and Susan wandered off searching for artefacts leaving me to scatter the carnations across the bunker. I spent some time studying the sheet of metal that had been its roof.

I reasoned that when the police had organised for the roof to be peeled off and tossed to one side, the inner side of the roof was thrown facing upward towards the sky. I got it into my head that if Barry had perished in the fire he would not have left without scratching a message to me somewhere. The soft underside of the metal roof seemed the best location. On hands and knees I studied each section in minute detail. I found nothing.

It was easy to convince myself that this proved that Barry had not been in the bunker when the fire came through. Yet his car was here at the property. In the shock of seeing the destruction at Waldene on my previous visit I had not noticed the twisted lump of rusted metal that had been Barry's Commodore. It was part way up the driveway, not in its usual parking space. But today as we had walked down the driveway I had recognised the burnt-out shell as a car. Why would the car still be here? I wondered. Why was it not parked where it normally was and why was it facing towards the house instead of towards the road like Barry always parked? Perhaps its gas tank had exploded, causing it to spin around and away from the house.

No message on the bunker roof and the car still at the property – I struggled with an impending sense of foreboding. What might the unusual location of the car mean?

It was over four years later that I suddenly realised the stupidity of my thinking that in such a holocaust, with only precious minutes available and fearing for his life, Barry would have taken the time to find something to stand on so that he could scratch a message to me on the underside of the bunker roof.

We stayed at Waldene for a few hours. It was a warm, sunny day and the yellow carnations lay suffering on the ground. Their slow death in this stark landscape seemed almost significant of my world and everything in it at that time. I sat for a long time in the hollow that marked where the bunker had been. I was trying to feel Barry beneath me somewhere. Surely this small piece of soil would be somehow different from everywhere else. Perhaps I just needed to sit here for a bit longer and things would sort themselves out.

My thinking swung backwards and forwards ... What should I do next? Why should I do anything? The ground is so black. There is no noise here; it is absolutely silent. There are no leaves, no branches, to rustle in the breeze. The birds have all gone. Surely this is a place of death ... yet the sun is shining and it is warm on my face. It is so very peaceful just sitting here in silence with Barry. Perhaps I could just sit here forever. Would it matter if I did?

Susan and Katie called me back. It was time to go, yet again. Not for the last time in the years that followed was I to wish that everyone else would just go and leave me here, sitting at the bunker waiting.

Later that afternoon, back at Greensborough, my friend Lynne and her husband came to visit. They brought with them a huge Italian homemade fruit cake that had been baked by a teacher, Carmela, with whom I had worked some years ago. Lynne, who is also a teacher, had mentioned at her school that she was coming to visit me and somehow through the teacher network Carmela had contacted Lynne and asked her to deliver the cake to me on her behalf; yet another of many, many kindnesses that I was to receive from an army of acquaintances and complete strangers in the years ahead.

Lynne gave me a beautiful, leather-bound writing book. A long leather strap wrapped around to hold it closed. She said that she wanted me to write about my love for Barry. She said that she had bought it because the wrap-around strap made her think of Barry's arms wrapping around me. It was a lovely sentiment and I was warmed to hear her talk about my love for Barry out loud. Somehow hearing it said by someone other than me confirmed its truth in the world.

Lynne's husband, Pete, is a member of the CFA and was on duty the night of the fires. He had been faced with the horrible task of answering phone calls from terrified residents screaming for the CFA to come and help them. His CFA depot had sent every truck as well as a makeshift trailer carting water barrels out to fight the fires. Pete had little to offer the many callers, other than the promise that the CFA were doing everything that they could and that help was on its way. But the situation was out of control. I listened to his tale with great sadness. I felt that he was somehow trying to apologise to me for Barry's loss.

I remember rising to the surface of my personal mental stupor for a moment to speak quietly and directly to Pete. I assured him that there was no way that anyone could have anticipated the ferocity of that fire. The dry summer, the fierce winds, the heat of the day all contributed to the making of a catastrophic circumstance that had never happened before and hopefully will never happen again. Nature was to blame for the fire, not the CFA or the government or the people themselves. I said that 'blame' should not be levelled at anyone. The fire was out of control and nature helped it to tear across the hills taking everything and everyone in its path. I reassured Pete that what was amazing to me was that when everyone else turns and runs from fire, the CFA people jump onto a truck and drive towards it – and they are volunteers! No-one forces them to drive into that mayhem. They choose to because they care. How could they feel blame in any of this?

Sunday 15 February 2009
Judy's partner, Jeff, and my son Heath arrived at Greensborough early to take me to Waldene to collect the table setting from the secret garden and to help move some of the heavier debris so that we could search beneath. Susan and Katie opted to remain at Greensborough. I was uncertain whether to go in Jeff's small truck or with Heath in his car. I felt obliged to both of them and did not want to hurt either man's feelings. Out of respect for the fact that Jeff was not a family member and yet had come to help, I asked Heath if it would be all right if I travelled with Jeff. He kindly agreed and said that that he would follow behind in his car.

On the drive to Waldene, Jeff asked how I was coping and what I was feeling. I sobbed for much of the telling and spoke of the pointlessness of my life without Barry.

Jeff said he believed that life is a sort of spinning wheel, like a merry-go-round. He said that at different times the wheel stops and people get on and others get off and then the wheel spins again. He described it as an inevitable process and to try to get off the wheel before your turn upsets the natural balance of things.

He spoke softly and convincingly. 'You may not think you can go on, but you can get through it and one day the wheel will stop and then it will be your turn.'

I suggested that Barry might expect me to choose to follow him right now and to do otherwise would disappoint him. Jeff assured me that I would be letting Barry down if I took the easy way out and hopped off the spinning wheel before my allotted time and left everything in the mess that it currently was.

I was unsure that I believed him, but his words gave me pause for thought. We drove on in meditative silence.

At Waldene, Heath and Jeff worked tirelessly loading the garden setting onto Jeff's truck before turning their attention to retrieving the cast iron stove that sat inside the stone chimney. I had expressed concern about the possibility that it might be stolen by looters if it remained at the site. Goodness knows what Jeff and Heath thought about the likelihood of this happening, but regardless, they directed their energies to retrieving the stove for me. It took them over an hour to free the stove and to lift its enormous weight up onto the truck.

We spent more time moving some of the heavy debris and searching beneath. Jeff was delighted when he found more broken pieces of fairy figurines from the white room. With great care he collected over a dozen pieces and put them in a bag for me; a sad collection of tiny limbs and faces and wings.

I wandered aimlessly around the site, standing to stare at the burnt-out frame of Barry's bicycle, a twisted metal candelabra, some cutlery, a biscuit tin full of rusting Meccano pieces. I laid out an odd assortment of relics on the concrete steps that used to lead from the garden into the billiard room. The items lay there exposed to the heat of the day – corpses on a peculiar slab in a forest morgue.

I found some billiard balls. They had lost all their outer gloss and were now a crumbling soft white powder around some hard inner core. I gathered up four to give to Steve as a memento of the tournaments that he had enjoyed so much.

There appeared at first glance to be nothing left of the rose garden. Years ago Barry had built a small wired-in enclosure about 2 metres square and filled it with a mixture of climbing and bush roses. A wire door opened onto a tiny paved area inside the 'cage' where one could stand and admire the roses. The day Barry had finished the rose garden we had hung a 'Fairy Garden' plaque on one wall and then made love on the little paved area. It was a magical place.

I stood on the paved area, which was all that remained now, and wished myself back to that day. I bent down close to the ground to see if perhaps one of the roses had somehow managed to avoid the carnage. I pushed the twisted wire mesh aside as I scoured from corner to corner, poking and prodding at the blackened soil as I went.

Then suddenly, there beneath some wire, covered in black soot, yet fully intact, appeared the 'Fairy Garden' wall plaque. It was a miracle. I let out a cry of joy. Surely this was a sign. The plaque appeared to have merely slipped from its location on the cage wall to land on the powdery ash below. There it had stayed as all hell had roared over it and there it had remained until I found it. I felt amazingly uplifted. I was convinced that somehow Barry had struck a deal somewhere that allowed me to have at least this one item returned to me intact. Of all the items that he could have bartered for, this one spoke of childish beliefs, of love, of joy and of our times together. It was wonderful. I carried the plaque on my lap all the way home. I placed it tenderly on a table top and to this day I remain too scared to risk hanging it up again.

That night I was visited by another brother, Victor, and his wife Karen. When Victor stepped into the kitchen I was shocked by how overcome with emotion I became. I leapt to my feet and fell into his arms. I felt a floodgate open inside me and I cried and cried into his chest. There is something about family that makes everything different. Perhaps it is because family knows everything you have had to endure in your life, everything you have done wrong, everything you missed out on, everything you overcame. They hold the 'sum' of you and can weigh up the enormity of one situation on your life in comparison to another. Perhaps it was that. Perhaps it was because I rarely see Victor and that a visit from him meant the loss of Barry was to be taken seriously, that there was probably no room for doubt now. I am not sure what I was thinking specifically, but the sight of Victor brought me tumbling down and it was some minutes before I could regain any sort of composure.

6

Monday 16 February 2009

Detective Cartagena arrived at Greensborough with another police officer and a female counsellor. They said they had driven in an unmarked car to save me from neighbourhood curiosity. I remember thinking how kind it was that someone somewhere had thought from that perspective amidst all the logistics associated with gathering information from hundreds of people about the fires. It seemed like a tiny piece of 'sensible' in a swirl of chaos.

We sat at the kitchen table. Detective Cartagena seemed nervous. Probably the sight of me clutching my pillow did not help the situation. He talked about the picturesque view from the kitchen window, about the terrible heat and he apologised for interrupting my day. He introduced his colleagues, whose names I cannot recall. The counsellor sat watching me for the next three hours. She did not say a word all that time, other than to respond when initially introduced by Detective Cartagena. With hindsight I imagine she was fairly traumatised by her role. The police force would have had to assemble a large collection of counsellors in a very short time frame for this task. Perhaps this counsellor was more accustomed to counselling people with dietary issues, behaviour problems or sleep disorders. At such short notice, where would they have been able to find a group of counsellors skilled at dealing with this horror?

Detective Cartagena said that he would do the questioning and that the other police officer would take notes. He explained that the police needed to identify missing people and match their details against any items or remains that had been recovered.

It was a difficult task, he said. I explained that I had given Barry's dental records to Daniel. He said that the dental records would be collected and put with my statements and any other statements relative to Barry's case.

I wondered fleetingly why Daniel had insisted that I give the dental records to him when it appeared that I could have given them directly to Detective Cartagena. Someone from the Phoenix Taskforce headquarters in Melbourne would now have to drive hours out into the country to collect the dental records. I was cross that this might delay the police finding Barry and/or identifying his body if he had perished in the fire.

Detective Cartagena apologised again because he had to ask me some specific questions about Barry; about his clothing and hair colour and so on. He said some of the questions were a bit personal and he was sorry about that but it was the only way the police and the Coroner could be sure they made the correct identifications. He said that because Australia had not had such a natural disaster of this proportion before, the police had elected to use the questionnaire that was developed to cope with the identification process after the 2007 tsunami in Indonesia.

I listened to what Detective Cartagena had to say with something approaching happiness. Surely he was hinting at the fact that the police had recovered some bodies but needed extra help to identify them. Perhaps if Barry had not survived the fire, somewhere his body was waiting to be identified and claimed. The police must have removed his body from the bunker and taken it to the morgue. I was anxious to tell them every single thing I knew about Barry's body, his clothing; anything they wanted to know, I would tell them. I knew every inch of his beautiful body. I knew what he wore and even what brand he wore. At last, here was something worthwhile that I could do to speed up Barry's return to me.

Detective Cartagena worked his way through the questionnaire, encouraging me to include as much detail in my answers as I could. How old was Barry, height, weight, dentures? Barry wore blue jeans, always the King Gee brand. He wore blue flannelette shirts in winter and blue short-sleeved cotton shirts in summer. On weekends and casual days he wore blue polo shirts. Barry wore brown leather shoes and blue woollen jumpers. With the exception of a few white singlets, all his underwear was navy blue; Bonds cotton brand. He wore navy blue socks; wool or wool blend. When the washing was on the line at Waldene at the end of the week there were fourteen identical navy blue socks hanging by one peg each, seven pairs of navy underpants and seven navy singlets. I used to laugh at Barry and say that it was as if the seven dwarfs were living at the cottage. He said that having identical socks was expedient because he never had to fuss about matching up pairs. He was so practical, so funny.

'Jewellery?'

'A watch on a thick silver band, worn on his left arm. He turned the clock face inwards rather than outwards. This was so that when he was sitting at his desk writing or correcting papers he could just glance at his left arm on the desk and see what time it was without having to turn his arm. Everything he did was sensible and had been thought through.' Detective Cartagena must have heard the admiration in my descriptions. I was so very proud of Barry. He was someone we should all aspire to be like.

'Any other jewellery?' Detective Cartagena asked. I described Barry's thick silver neck chain. When I first met Barry I had thought that the neck chain was somewhat out of character for him. I had always associated neck chains with playboy types and

Barry was certainly not of that ilk. Yet, there it was; he always wore that neck chain. Perhaps it was because he liked jewellery per se. He used to buy me expensive jewellery, but I was usually too scared to wear it for fear of losing it. He thought I was silly. He had never met a girl who preferred shiny plastic baubles to expensive jewels. He kidded me about it but I know he also liked my lack of greed and pretentiousness.

Barry's silver neck chain was loose enough that it draped across my lips when we made love. I showed the forensic group the silver bracelet that Barry had bought me some years ago. It was a reminder of that silver neck chain and our love-making.

The questioning eventually moved away from Barry's clothing to an interrogation of his naked body. I enjoyed describing his beautiful form to them. I murmured on, almost to myself, about his broad strong back, about his huge hands and thick solid fingers. I spoke of the muscular calves that he had developed through decades of amateur cycling events. I hated his toes. Ingrown toenails that had been removed leaving tiny chips of nail stumps in their stead.

Detective Cartagena apologised again and asked me if Barry was circumcised. I was conscious of the eyes of the counsellor watching me. 'Other distinguishing body marks or features?' On and on we went. I did not tire of the interview. In answering their questions my mind was allowed the pleasure of inspecting every small centimetre of my darling boy. I saw the blue of his eyes as I stared into his face, I saw the bulge of his calves as he strode ahead of me in his shorts on our many bushwalks, I felt the breadth of his chest as he held me against him, I smelt the shampoo he used as we showered together.

Surely they had found a body. This amount of detailed information was indicative that there was somewhere a body to be compared to my description. Detective Cartagena said that they were also interested in anything that I could tell them about Barry and about Waldene that would help them piece together what might have happened on Black Saturday. Once again I repeated what I had now told many times over since the fires. Every so often Detective Cartagena interrupted me to ask for extra information or to clarify some point. He asked me to describe what sort of person Barry was. He wondered how well prepared he was for fires at Waldene.

He asked about the bunker. Some of his questions were puzzling. I asked why he needed me to describe the bunker when the police had already seen it themselves. Detective Cartagena said that he had not personally been to Waldene. His role was to take detailed statements from people and that the information would then be passed on to the Phoenix Taskforce. There were many people to be interviewed and the police wanted to collect the information as close as possible to when the fire had occurred. This meant that other police were being used to do the interviews on behalf of the Phoenix Taskforce.

After almost three hours, and a few cups of tea and slices of Carmela's fruit cake, the interview ended. All the information was to be typed into a report and someone would come back and read it through with me to make sure it was correct before I signed it. We all shook hands and the group left.

Later that afternoon Susan left me in Katie's care to return home. At some stage I realised that my mobile phone contained a few unanswered voice messages from earlier days. The first was a message from Judy a few days earlier advising me she would be delayed arriving. The second message both shocked and delighted me: Barry's voice! He had called me some days earlier. I listened in awe. He spoke in a whining sort of tone, obviously meaning to be funny.

'Hello … I called you on both phines/phones/lines … What am I trying to say? … phones. I don't know where you are. Oh my God! I don't know what to do… Bye.'

Followed by a long, juicy kissing noise.

I let out a shout and Katie came running to see what was wrong. She found me grinning from ear to ear.

'It's Barry. He's on my phone. He left me a message,' I beamed. Katie was incredulous.

'I think he left it on the day of the fire. He must have been trying to call me while I was at work. I had my phone turned off,' my words tumbled out.

I held the phone up and we both listened in silence as the message replayed. There he was, larger than life, funny and alive, almost a tangible presence in the room. I felt deliriously happy. I wanted to play the call over and over again, but at the same time I was frightened that I would somehow push the wrong button on the phone and inadvertently delete the message completely.

Katie and I sat grinning at each other. It was a wonderful moment amidst all the grief and sorrow of the past week. We talked about how we might be able to preserve the voice message somehow. Katie felt sure that the telecommunications service automatically deletes voice messages after a certain number of days.

She phoned her husband, Rob, who used to work for Vodaphone. He confirmed that voice messages are deleted sometime after a week. That meant that if Barry had made the call on 7 February (Black Saturday), the voice message might be deleted as early as today. Rob suggested that Katie phone Telstra and explain the situation and that they might be able to circumvent the automatic deletion process. Katie rang and spoke to a Telstra operator who said they would try to override the process.

I phoned Detective Cartagena in the hopes that the police might be able to lift the message off the phone and transfer it to a CD for me. The detective was interested to hear about the voice message. I noted his concern when I relayed what Barry had said in the message. I realised that taken out of context, the detective thought the words were made by Barry when he was trapped by the fire. I quickly explained that Barry's voice tone was one of humour, suggesting that the recording had been made well before the advent of the fire.

Relieved, Detective Cartagena said that he would arrange for the phone to be picked up. He asked me to write an authorisation giving him permission to access the phone's data. I typed out the permission and listened to Barry's voice once more, taking extra pains to ensure I did nothing to delete the message. Katie and I went to bed full of optimism that I would soon have a permanent recording of Barry speaking directly to me.

Tuesday 17 February 2009
Upon waking the following morning, I reached for my mobile phone. Barry's voice message was gone! I struggled for air. Had I somehow deleted the message myself? Had the Telstra operator erroneously deleted it while trying to save it? Had the Telstra operator not even tried to override the automatic delete? Once again, I felt myself a pawn on some cruel emotional roller-coaster. Yesterday I had been presented with this most wonderful find, only to have it snatched away before I could enjoy it in full. Had I known that the message would be gone with the arrival of the dawn, I would have defied sleep and listened to it over and over throughout the night.

I called Katie and we sat together, bereft at this latest blow.

Between us we worked out that Barry must have left the message the evening before Black Saturday when he was trying to contact me about what we were going to have for dinner. The call would have been made at about 5 pm on Friday 6 February. Seven days later would have meant it was due to be deleted any time after 5 pm on the 13th. The fact that the message had remained on the phone until I had found it on the 16th was nothing short of a miracle. Yet, seeing my renewed distress, some would suggest that it would have been kinder if the message had deleted automatically without me ever knowing of its existence.

Wednesday 18 February 2009
The detectives interviewed me again for another couple of hours in order to add further information to that given in the previous interview. I was shown a map and asked to mark the back roads that I had taken when trying to get through to Barry after the fires. I also sketched a map showing the layout of the property including the bunker, house, sheds and water tanks. There was still no information about Barry's whereabouts other than the mention that 'remains' had been located in the bunker. Talking to the detectives was almost a relief, somehow serving to keep Barry here with me, alive in the present. It was with some sadness that I finally bade them goodbye.

Thursday 19 February 2009
A large envelope arrived by mail from Daniel. He advised me that he had 'everything under control re the memorial service' and included a coloured copy of 'the printed material that will be available on the 25th'. His letter went on to advise me that he had yesterday 'signed papers re: the undertaker and the assignment of

the Remains and Ashes to my care'.

Apparently I was not to be involved in planning Barry's memorial service and additionally it was evident that Daniel was resolved to ignore my fervent requests to be given the ashes. His letter seemed totally devoid of warmth.

The printed material that he planned to distribute at the memorial service turned out to be a one-page flyer that he had created on his home computer. I thought it looked like the 'Missing' posters that people nail to poles when their pet disappears. The photo of Barry on the top page dated back eleven years, just after he had shaved off his usual thick moustache. It didn't look like Barry. The text listed Daniel as 'friend' ahead of me as 'partner' and provided a program for the service including music Daniel had selected. This was followed by a set of rules for how the service would be conducted. I thought it was an awful document lacking in any dignity or style. I was appalled that Barry would be represented by such a document.

I phoned Daniel. Sharna answered the phone and I explained my concerns. Daniel was apparently sitting across the room from her. She turned away from the phone to tell him that I did not like the photo. I heard Daniel call out from his seat, 'What do you want me to do; draw a moustache on him?'

I was shocked at his insensitivity. I suggested to Sharna that they use a different photo. Again she conveyed the information to Daniel, who for reasons best known to himself, still opted not to speak to me directly. He said that he did not have many photos of Barry; to which I replied that he should have asked me for some. Ignoring my offer, Daniel said he had already paid for multiple copies of the flyer to be printed in colour. His apparently offhand attitude towards me was upsetting.

I asked Sharna if I could nominate some music to be played

while people were entering the hall where the service was to be held. This seemed reasonable given that Daniel had listed three opera songs to be played during the service. Daniel told Sharna to tell me that he did not think we needed any extra music. Too upset to speak further, I ended the phone conversation. It seemed that for some reason my involvement in Barry's memorial service was to be minimal. I had the distinct feeling that Daniel was angry at me or perhaps jealous of Barry and my relationship. I could not fathom why this might be.

I sat alongside the phone sobbing. It seemed that even in this small matter of ensuring that the memorial service was worthy of the man, I was destined to let Barry down.

That night my youngest brother Neil and his wife Heather visited. We discussed the flyer that Daniel had created and I lamented my preference for something smaller and more refined. They suggested that I make up a version of what I would like instead, and then email it to Daniel for consideration. Later I worked on an alternative memorial card, hoping that Daniel would agree once he saw what I intended. I had nothing to lose.

Friday 20 February 2009
Early morning I sent an email to Daniel with my alternative card attached. I felt sure once he saw the card he would choose to use it instead of his flyer.

That morning I took Katie to the airport. She had already extended her stay beyond what she had originally intended. She was out of leave entitlements and had no option but to return home. Tears welled in my eyes as I hugged her at the airport. It was the first time that I would be alone since the fires. I felt suddenly small and weak. Katie hugged me and told me I would be all right.

I listened to her as a child listens to its mother explain nightmares away. She was a good friend and I knew she was worried about me.

I drove home and phoned the company that had created the memorial cards for my mother's funeral two years earlier. I wanted to ascertain if there was enough time for them to have 100 cards printed before Barry's memorial service on Wednesday. The company said that normally this would not be possible, but given the circumstances they could prioritise the order. They would require at least two days turnaround. The content and layout needed to be emailed to them as soon as possible. I hung up the phone feeling frantic. Time was growing short.

While I waited to hear from Daniel, I read and re-read the collection of cards and handwritten notes from Barry that I had collected in my pillowcase. Judy arrived to accompany me to a local theatre production. Barry and I had bought tickets for quite a number of plays and operas throughout the year ahead. I was not sure how I would manage these events; would I stay home or source various friends to sit alongside me in Barry's seat? It was too early to know, but tonight at least Judy had said she would come with me.

An hour before we were to leave for the theatre, I still had not heard back from Daniel. Judy told me to phone him. Feeling very anxious I dialled his number. He told me that he had not received the email. I quickly explained its contents and said that I would resend it. Once again I asked if I could nominate some music to begin the service. He said he would think on it.

Daniel then said that he had acquiesced to my request to organise for some food to be available to people after the service. I offered to pay him but he declined saying the cost would come from the estate. I resent the email to him, and Judy and I left for the theatre.

Saturday 21 February 2009

In the morning Daniel's reply arrived.

> *Dear Sue,*
>
> *I have taken into account all you said to me on the phone. There will be extra classical music (not opera) prior to the service … about 10 min and about another 10 min after the service.*
>
> *…. I will use a colour card system to see that significant persons get to speak during the service. I will brief a roving mike person to give certain people preference … not too many… as lots of others less known to us should also get a chance … it will all work out … trust me.*
>
> *The opera music is a very important part of the meditation and reflection time. I have chosen with great care and love … the time will fly. It's beautiful music … he would love it … Sorry can't change.*

Judy had stayed with me overnight. We sat together and talked over everything that was planned for the memorial service. It all seemed too awful to be true. How could Daniel be so stubborn and why was he marginalising me on every decision? Judy convinced me to stand up for myself. She said that if I wanted the small cards that I had created then I should organise to have them printed and just show up at the memorial service with them. After all, what could Daniel do about it? She was correct of course. I realised that Daniel was making all the decisions because I was letting him.

I decided that it was more important to me that Barry's memorial card did him justice than it was that people would be momentarily confused by the presence of two different handouts at the service. I phoned the card company and the man asked me to email the text and photos through to him and he would begin work immediately.

It was a great weight off my mind to know that I was going to 'win' this tiny battle.

I rewrote the text, deleting that which I had originally included to appease Daniel. The simple text now reflected only those things that I wanted to say. After some soul-searching I decided to put my name ahead of Daniel's on the card. It seemed bizarre that it should be any other way.

I also replaced the photo for one that Barry had posed for in 2008 when we went on a cruise. Never a tie wearer, he had bought a second-hand tie for the cruise when I had threatened to attend the Captain's dinner without him if he did not 'suit up'. It was funny to see how pleased he was with his debonair look in a jacket and tie. We had some photos taken together all dressed up and then he asked to have one taken by himself. He wanted it to send to his biological mother in Adelaide. He was very pleased with the photo and luckily I had made a copy for my office as well.

I emailed the information to the card company asking them to print 100 copies of the memorial cards and courier them back to me before Wednesday.

Sunday 22 February 2009
Judy left in the morning. I was to spend the day and night alone. We both cried as we hugged each other goodbye. It was a fortnight since the fires and it was now time for me to face the loneliness and the silence that would replace Barry's presence in my life. I waved Judy off and turned back to the empty house as one who stares down a long, long tunnel that leads to nowhere.

I spent the day crying.

Roused by the darkness of the night, I played the song 'Goodbye my lover' by James Blunt. This was the music that I had hoped Daniel would allow me to play prior to Barry's memorial service. I had taken to playing it repeatedly each night as I lay awake, clutching a photo of Barry and the two teddies Dekky and Stewie. Tonight, in the empty house, the music seemed sadder. I lay sobbing, wondering if I would survive and trying to decide if I even wanted to.

Monday 23 February 2009
My son Blake and his girlfriend returned home from their holiday in Bali. They came to visit me. I do not remember anything they told me about their time away and I can only guess what they thought when they saw me. We sat drinking tea in the kitchen and after some time they left to visit friends.

The phone rang throughout the day. I was now responsible for taking the calls myself. I spoke as an automaton, repeating facts and agreeing that I was 'doing well'; something most callers wanted to hear. This usually lasted for a few minutes until they sensed the silence at my end of the phone which was soon swamped by an enormous outburst of tears. The caller would mumble some commiseration and promise to phone me back at another time.

I tried to write a eulogy speech. I could not find the words. Everything seemed hard and clinical. The words about his life achievements made him sound like other people. I could not say words like that. Barry was much more than the people he mixed with, the politics he followed or the positions he had held. Where were the words that showed the person inside? I became distraught. I was a writer and yet I could not find the words. I wrote down the letters of the alphabet and stared at them. Somewhere in these 26 letters were 'the words'. Time was running out.

I went to Officeworks and made a large copy of the photo of

Barry wearing the tie and jacket and bought a frame to put it in. There needed to be a photo of Barry somewhere at the memorial service and I wanted it to be this one. I was not sure where the framed photo would be placed, given that there was no coffin. But I was happy to know that at least this photo would be on display at Trades Hall regardless of any photo Daniel might produce.

I wanted to wear a long patterned cheesecloth skirt to the memorial service. Barry and I had bought a set of these skirts for me when we were in Turkey a few years ago. Being cocooned inside the hippie skirt from waist to ankle would be comforting on the day; a protective layer around me. My red T-shirt was old and faded. I wanted Barry to be proud of me. I drove to the shopping centre, bought a long-sleeved T-shirt and hurried home. I must write the eulogy. The clock continued to tick.

I began thinking about how my sons and my ex-husband Alec would feel as they listened to me speak about how much and for how long I had been in love with Barry. This made finding the words I would speak at the memorial service even more difficult.

I sat for a long time thinking things through. My sons were grown up and living their own lives now. Alec also was now getting on with his own life. Barry and I had sacrificed many years to them all already. We had met secretly at first and always placed our needs after those of my family commitments, my sons, Alec and later my aged mother. On and on we had twisted and turned, stretched and squeezed our times together so that no-one else would be hurt or compromised. Barry had patiently waited and waited for me, thankful for any time we could have together. Even when our relationship became public, we had tiptoed around my family, trying not to upset anyone troubled by seeing me in any role other than their mother, their daughter, their sister, their ex-wife, etc.

And now, even here, at Barry's memorial service, I was worrying about upsetting these family members.

I made a decision. I phoned my youngest brother and asked him to distract Alec during my speech; perhaps he might even be able to distract my sons also. I was determined to say what I wanted to say without concern for their feelings. I wondered why it had taken Barry's death to make me see that people generally are resilient; had I just stood up and bared the situation years earlier, Barry and I might even have married and my family would have resolved themselves to it, sighed and gotten on with their own lives anyway. I was such a fool!

So the day crept on, to eventually flow into another dark night; the stillness broken only by the strains of James Blunt singing a sorrowful song to the accompaniment of my tortured, quiet sobbing.

Tuesday 24 February 2009

An email that I sent in response to a (distant) colleague's query about a work-related matter reveals something of my inner turmoil as this day dawned.

> *... have not been up to replying yet ... sorry. My partner's memorial service is to be held tomorrow (Wednesday 25th) and it's taking me all my energy and concentration to get to there. Once that's over somehow everything will be ... something! ... perhaps resolved, even sensible, definite, final, normal, bearable ... not sure what or why, but I am somehow hanging my hopes on that. It's taking a VERY long time to get from one milestone to the next in this tragedy. We still don't have a body or 'remains' ... that will come MUCH later the police tell me.*

I still had nothing on paper for a eulogy. Daniel rang to explain his plan for the day. The service would begin at 11 am and we were to vacate Trades Hall by 1.30 pm. Daniel had decided we would aim for about one hour for the service and one hour for refreshments afterwards. He would speak first. He had selected an opera piece to play as people moved into the hall, and also incorporated three opera pieces as part of his speech. During the music he would direct people to sit in silence and reflect on Barry's life. He said he needed about 20 minutes for his speech.

Then he would invite me to speak. He suggested I might speak for between five and ten minutes. I felt slighted at the imbalance between the time he had allocated between me and him. After I had spoken, people in the audience would be invited to speak into a portable microphone. He thought about five or six people each speaking for a few minutes would be sufficient. Then Daniel would close the service and invite people to enjoy the refreshments.

Daniel asked me what I was going to say. I said that I was not sure yet. He explained that he was going to describe Barry's life from his adoption as a baby, through to his time at teachers college, his involvement with the Draft Resisters' Union during the Vietnam era and all his work with the Trade Unions and schools. Daniel said that he would also talk about how much he would miss Barry and reminisce about some of the times they had shared together. I had the feeling that he was explaining that in fact he was going to cover everything and therefore perhaps he could justify the time allocation on this basis.

'I'm just warning you that there's some pretty emotional stuff in what I'm going to say,' Daniel finished. I thought how pathetic that was. Surely the very walls of Trades Hall would be bulging with 'emotional stuff' about Barry. When someone wonderful is taken, it cannot be anything but 'emotional'.

I told Daniel not to be concerned that there would be any overlap in our speeches. I had no intention of doing an historical perspective of Barry's life. I would leave the historical facts to Daniel and anyone from the Union or the education system who might speak at the service. I would only be talking about Barry and me together, as a couple. Anything I said would be only to describe our love and our life together.

I hung up the phone and pondered. What were the words? What would I say? Could it all be encapsulated within a ten-minute speech? Could I speak of the great depth and breadth of our love in front of a roomful of strangers? Barry was always a very private person. Would speaking about 'us' break some code of trust between Barry and I? But I did not want people to think Barry was only a teacher, or only a political agitator, or only a builder or a Collingwood football fan or an opera devotee or a bushwalker or avid reader. These features were good and honest but they described the 'outside Barry'. Who would speak for the 'inside Barry' if not me?

I thought and thought. I was ever conscious of the clock hands moving me towards tomorrow. Suddenly I saw what I needed to do. I had been thinking eulogy speech and along with this title came formal phrases like 'Ladies and gentlemen' and the checklist of achievements by which people rank the sum of a man's life. But Barry and I were not of this public domain. We lived hidden away in the forest. Ours was a fairy tale. Why not write a fairy tale instead of a eulogy? The words would come easier, more natural, more like us and how we were together. Tell them about the beauty and magic of 'us'. Leave others to describe the ordinary outer shell of 'my' Barry.

I wrote with joy. The words tumbled out and organised themselves upon the page. I could see sunshine and rainbows and hear giggling and smell flowers. It was a tale of our love. I stopped writing when the words stopped. It was brief but it said all that was needed.

I had never been strong enough to read or speak at a funeral service. Always I have had to pass my written speech to a celebrant or family member to deliver on my behalf. I have always been too emotional, too sensitive. Barry liked that about me. 'You're such a little mouse,' he used to gently tease me.

I went in search of the drugs prescribed by the doctor when Judy had forced me to attend the clinic after the fires. I read the label. I decided to take one tablet in the morning. It would help calm me. Then I would talk slowly and I would say this speech at the memorial service even if it took me an hour and was full of long tear-filled interludes. I was resolved that I must tell the world about the 'inside Barry.' I did not want him to be remembered as a set of ticks on a checklist. He was so much more than people could imagine. Perhaps they would not understand? It did not matter. I just needed to say it and then I would know that it had been said.

Alec phoned. He apologised but said he had decided not to attend the memorial service. I wondered if this was a result of contact from my youngest brother. I was greatly relieved. He offered to prepare food for people to have back at the house in Greensborough after the memorial service. I accepted his offer with gratitude, having not even thought this far ahead until now. I offered to leave the key in a secret location and we discussed what catering he might organise.

The mail contained an A4-sized notice from Victoria Police. The thick black lettering and the simple text all but shouted a word of warning:

AFFECTED FIRE AREA
NO CLEAN UP OF SITES

until the Coroner, on advice from Victoria Police, approves access to the site following the reasonable search of all affected properties.

I was finally allowed into Waldene, but now I was not allowed to rescue anything that I might find there. It was hard enough to wander around the ruin that was all that remained of my life with Barry, but now I was forbidden from moving anything or taking away anything for safekeeping. I abandoned myself once again to crying. I was powerless in all things. How could Barry have ever fallen in love with me? I had never felt so useless!

Late in the afternoon the memorial cards arrived by courier from the printer. They were in a little cardboard box. They looked beautiful. I carried the box around with me from room to room, suddenly protective of these 100 tiny images of Barry.

7

Wednesday 25 February 2009

Judy arrived early. She had insisted on driving me to the service. I felt a fleeting guilt when I explained this to my sons when they phoned to ask how I was going to get to Trades Hall. It was a relief to know that driving to the service I would just be with Judy. She understood my silences, fears and grief.

I told Judy that I had written a fairy tale for my eulogy speech. She looked concerned. I said that I had to write it that way. It was the only thing that made sense to me. I showed Judy the three pages of typed text. I had printed it in a large-sized font so that I would be able to see it more easily if I began to cry during its reading.

Judy sat quietly and read my words. When she had finished she looked up at me, smiled and said, 'That's perfect.'

I put the pages inside a plastic pocket. I added one of Barry's handkerchiefs, my reading glasses and Stewie, the tiny teddy. I was not going to take anything except the large framed photo of Barry, the box of memorial cards and the plastic pocket. I did not want any complications.

I showed Judy the box of cards from the publisher. As I handed one of the cards to her I felt an enormous heartache. I looked at the photo of Barry on the card that Judy was holding. I could imagine everyone walking away from the memorial service taking that photo with them. I suddenly did not want anyone to have the photo. Barry had been snatched away from me and now people would take his photo from me as well. I told Judy that I did not think I could give the cards out.

She remained calm. She told me that I could decide when I arrived at the memorial service. I took the tablet prescribed by the doctor. Then, picking up the box of cards, Barry's framed photo and the plastic pocket, we left. It was almost 10 am and the service was to begin at 11 am.

Inside Trades Hall, Judy dropped the bombshell that she would be 'floating around' if I needed her, but that she would not be sitting next to me for the service. She said that my eldest brother Richard should sit with me. I glanced across the rows of seats facing the stage. Here and there a familiar face. I felt myself shaking. I needed to get control of myself. I would not let Barry down.

Some large A5 posters of Barry had been stuck around the wall at eye height. The top of the page bore the red Trades Hall logo. Barry's smiling face looked out between two slashes of thick black computer type. Above Barry's head was printed the single word VALE, while across the bottom he was identified as BARRY JOHNSTON.

It was a photo that I had not seen before and yet it looked a fairly recent shot. It had obviously been snapped without giving Barry notice, because in the photo he was wearing his glasses. Barry always made a point of removing his glasses for photos; some rule his mother had taught him as a boy. His flannelette shirt and jumper suggested that it had probably been taken in the cooler months. I wondered if it was taken at his last union meeting before retiring in early September 2004. I made a mental note to ask someone if I could have one (all) of the posters at the conclusion of the service.

I walked down to examine a huge spray of flowers atop a small table on the stage. A card on the flowers announced that they had been sent by Barry's 'cousin Alan'. I studied the card with undue concentration. I was trying to breathe, fighting a rising panic. I placed the framed photo beside the flowers and stared hard into Barry's smiling eyes. He was so serene. If I could just stand here and stare into his face, I might become calmer. I just needed to slow myself down, block out the background noise, shrink the past and the near future until they did not exist; just stand and look into Barry's face and feel his calmness.

I glanced around. Kayleen, a long-time girlfriend since my childhood, had flown down from Queensland for the memorial service. She was standing alone against a side wall watching me. I burst into tears. Kayleen hurried over and hugged me in the soothing, murmuring manner that old friends invariably adopt.

Daniel appeared at my side. I showed him the cards that I had organised. He said, 'They look good. Do you want me to put them up near the sign-in book?' I assumed his 'flyers' were stacked there already. I tried to explain that now I was uncertain that I wanted people to have the cards. I said that Barry looked so lovely in the photo that I was not sure that I could part with them. Daniel convinced me that this was probably not a good idea. Reluctantly I gave him the cards and he moved away.

Someone ushered me into a seat in the front row between Richard and Daniel. I was sure that Judy had pushed Richard to sit next to me in case I faltered during my speech and he was needed to take over.

The crowd of over 200 moved in to fill the seats and become a press of people standing around the walls of the hall. After one glance over my shoulder I was too frightened to look back again in case I broke down.

Daniel began his speech. He spoke loudly and clearly. His speech matched the historical description he had shared with me on the phone. He mentioned what colour shoes and socks Barry wore when he was a youngster, said that Barry had loved going to the movies and he even listed the different rooms at Waldene. It all seemed very clinical. Every so often he paused to take a few deep breaths. He was either wrestling with his emotions or invoking dramatic effect. My concentration faded in and out as he spoke. Music welled up and then more talking. I was focused on trying to remain calm. My hands continued to shake.

It seemed as though the final part of Daniel's speech were perhaps aimed most directly at me. Taken from the printed version he later gave me, his speech ended with the following:

'In closing I wish to say that there will be no further public service or funeral. Barry's remains will be privately cremated in Ballarat. His ashes will be returned to me so we can take him to his final resting place according to his will and wishes. Please be assured that Barry will be at rest just the way he wanted it.

I would like to call on Sue now to speak about her memories and love for Barry.'

I felt my insides lurch. Daniel stepped away from the microphone and came down the stairs to sit beside me. I looked at the stairs and the stage. Could I do it?

I got to my feet clutching the plastic pocket. Slowly I moved up the stairs. Behind me the hall was hushed. I could hear my heart pounding in my chest. Once behind the podium I looked up. There was a sea of faces and I felt very, very small. The spotlight on the stage seemed painfully bright.

I took the items from the plastic pocket. I put on my reading glasses and the crowd mercifully blurred. I spread out the three pages, gripped Stewie in one hand, the scrunched handkerchief in the other. I glanced up and spoke my first words without realising. They deviated from what I had written. I said, 'I have had some drugs ... so I should be able to do this.' It was my inner self begging the audience to be patient with me. At the time I did not realise how dreadful this opening statement must have sounded. It is a credit to the audience that no-one laughed. Perhaps the tragic image that I presented meant that my words merely conveyed the obvious.

I swung my eyes back to the pages spread before me. Like a student learning to read, I dragged a finger along under the text to keep me going. A few times, leaving my finger marking the point on the page, I looked up and ad libbed some words to better explain a point. I remember seeing Barry's 'cousin Jill' in the audience. She seemed to be sitting very upright in her seat concentrating hard on what I was saying. Thereafter, whenever I looked up, I looked at her. It was easier than engaging with the enormous crowd.

I read on slowly; as loudly as I could. My lowered head was focused solely on the page before me. I really, really wanted to do this for Barry and for myself. The room full of people remained totally silent. I struggled on, every so often pausing to mop the flow of tears on my cheeks or to wipe my nose. I remember concentrating hard. I felt short of breath but I went on and on until I had read every word.

Just before I was to read a concluding poem, 'Colours' by Yevtushenko, I looked up at the audience. Until then I had been reading to myself and to Barry, and suddenly I had just realised something. I said aloud to the audience, 'I needed Barry but the fact that he gave me this poem a long time ago maybe showed that he needed me too.' I am sure that my sense of amazement at this revelation was evident in my voice. Barry had needed me. How wonderful it was to know that.

The end of the poem ended my speech. The audience waited. I was exhausted. Ludicrously I mumbled '... and I'm sorry, Daniel, but that's all I have to say'. I stepped down from the stage. I was uncertain if it took me five minutes or five hours to deliver my speech, but I had done it.

Following is an excerpt from my speech. The ad libbed lines were few and not clearly remembered so therefore not included.

> My name is Sue. Many of you may not know me or even know of me. I am Barry's partner. We didn't live together but it is truer to say that we didn't live apart. In a cruel act of fate I wasn't in my usual place, beside him, on February 7th.
>
> Barry and I were in love for a long, long time. My circumstances meant that much of our relationship involved waiting – waiting until other people's needs were met. As a result we spent most of our time together beyond the public gaze ... just Barry and I ... willing prisoners in a secret, magical world of our own making.
>
> Barry gave me the bounteous gifts of knowledge and courage and boundless love. In return I gave him fairy tales and laughter and my eternal love.
>
> I don't want to talk about all the things that the 'public' Barry stood for and represented – I will leave that for others to say.
>
> Instead I want to tell you about 'my' Barry. It's a fairy tale about a nondescript girl who met a gentle man. The girl was small and insignificant – hidden from life. The gentle man heard her silent voice. He took her hand and led her into a secret garden. He strewed the ground with flowers and made her picnics. He lent her books and he read her poetry. They talked and talked until the stars came out above the garden. Yet on they talked; together ... together ... both wishing the night was never done.

They talked of music, of history, of art and he stroked her hair. He brought her gifts to make her smile – buttons and toys, jewels and music-boxes. She kissed his lips and filled his dreams. They scribed love letters to each other and he built her a tower. He named her his princess and she dubbed him her librarian.

At times the pair left the secret garden to travel to faraway lands. He held her aloft that she might see the world better. He showed her palaces and snow-capped mountains and blue-veined cities. They wandered hand-in-hand through museums and along winding cobbled lanes. They shared secrets, created a history and painted each other's dreams. She loved him completely and he loved her equally in return.

Barry's love was 'life' to me.

I had wished for a happy ending to my fairy tale. Instead I now have to be content to hold Barry locked inside my heart forever – a never-ending love story.

Barry now waits patiently for me once again; a lonely sentinel at the door of my heart … my beautiful boy.

Daniel resumed his position at the podium and explained the roving microphone concept to the audience. I watched appalled as he directed the microphone to first be given to his wife. Sharna expressed similar sentiments to what we had already heard from Daniel with regard to her memories of Barry and what she would miss about him.

The microphone was then given to the wife of a friend of Barry's from teachers college days. I wondered why she spoke instead of her husband. Many people in the audience signalled that they wanted to speak.

Daniel gestured for the microphone to be passed on. An old

stalwart from the Labor Party spoke of a sixteen-year-old Barry arriving at his door asking to join the Labor Party. A social worker spoke of Barry's work as a volunteer delegate in East Timor in 1999 during the Popular Consultation process that formed part of that country's election process.

Pam, an old girlfriend of Barry's from when he was in his twenties, spoke. I cannot remember what she said but she later sent me a card in which she had written the following lovely words: 'It is a very fine man we have lost ... I'm proud to have known him and will try to honour him by borrowing a little of his spirit.' I imagine her speech reflected that sentiment.

A musical director of national acclaim spoke and attributed much of his success to Barry's encouragement of him when he first demonstrated his musical bent as a student in Barry's class at primary school. Barry would have been very interested to hear what impact he had on all these people from many walks of life. I was so proud for him.

Daniel interrupted some speakers telling them that they needed to be briefer. Although necessary, this seemed fairly insensitive and dictatorial. After this handful of speeches, Daniel reclaimed the stage, directed us to listen to yet another opera piece and then formally ended the service.

I was corralled by a line of wellwishers as I moved towards the anteroom where refreshments were being served. Many of the women came to tell me how much they had enjoyed my speech. They described it as lovely and romantic. Some shook my hand and told me I was brave. One man said it was easy to see why Barry was in love with me.

Someone handed me a cup of tea when it became obvious that I was not going to make it into the anteroom. I shook hands with people, thanked them for coming and accepted their murmured compliments and condolences. Some of the people I knew, but most were strangers to me. There were very old men in suits, jean-clad teenagers and shy, nervous children in primary school uniforms. There were men and women and boys and girls. The sea of people ebbed and flowed between the main hall and the anteroom.

Barry's stepbrother, Mark, from Adelaide, pushed into my view to offer his condolences. He had brought Barry's birth mother to the service. She was apparently somewhere out in the crowd of people. During our brief conversation Mark commented on a small photo of Waldene that Barry had sent to his birth mother some years ago. Mark's description of the photo matched a photo that had hung beside the front door at Waldene. I asked if he could make me a copy of the photo as I was now reduced to the one photo of Waldene; that which featured on the memorial card. It seemed a blessing when Mark agreed to post me a copy on his return to Adelaide.

Mark moved along, to be replaced by other people in the line. At one point, someone touched my arm and gestured me towards a woman standing off to my side. 'Do you know who this is?' I was asked.

'No,' I said, offering a small smile of apology.

'It's Barry's sister Judith,' the person murmured. Judith took a step forward as if to hug me. Involuntarily, I took a step back and Judith stopped in her tracks. I was in a mental fog but I knew that Barry had insisted that she not be involved in his funeral. I knew this and she knew this and yet here she was. Not only that, she was making the enormous assumption that she and I shared some bond.

I turned back to the line of people who were still waiting to speak to me, the misplaced smile still frozen on my face. I had not said anything to Judith. I could not believe that she was there, let alone that she had orchestrated for someone to direct my attention to her presence.

Soon after, Daniel appeared at my side and said that they were cleaning up in the anteroom. He said that there were some photos of Barry, taken as part of a union crowd, on display in the anteroom. A Trade Union photographer had provided them and told Daniel that I could keep them if I wanted them. I said that I did want them as well as any of the A5 posters of Barry in the main hall.

Judy drove Kayleen, Richard and me back to Greensborough. True to his promise Alec greeted us with finger food and drinks. Daniel and Sharna had followed Judy back and another handful of close friends and relations arrived soon after.

It was at this gathering that I asked Daniel about Barry's sister's attendance at the memorial service. He admitted that she had phoned him and asked if she could attend. Daniel had explained to her that Barry had expressly requested that she not be at his funeral; however, he had weakened and said she could come. Once again I wondered why Daniel was prepared to be flexible about some parts of Barry's instructions but not other parts. Why could Judith attend the service and yet I was to be denied the ashes?

Before leaving, Daniel handed me a large envelope containing a typed copy of his eulogy speech and a copy of the flyer he had distributed at the memorial service. He proudly announced that after speaking with me on the phone he had swapped the original photo of Barry for another photo he had found.

Later when I opened the envelope, I was pleased with the new photo of Barry on the revised flyer although I felt it still resembled a 'Missing' poster and lacked any dignity.

Most surprising was the inclusion of what I think was intended as a cover sheet of the envelope's contents. It held an awkward photo of Barry with Sharna and another photo of Barry standing in Daniel's shadow. The envelope also contained a CD of the opera music played during the service. I suppose he meant well, but he just seemed unable to see things through any eyes other than his own.

One by one everyone left until there was only Kayleen and Richard left. We sat talking until after midnight. When we all finally went to bed I felt as if a huge weight had been lifted from my shoulders. I no longer needed to find the words. I had said all that I needed to say.

PART 2

STOLEN

8

Thursday 26 February 2009
After breakfast Richard explained that he had been in contact with people supporting victims of the bushfires. He had told them about Daniel's determination to scatter Barry's ashes against my wishes. The bushfire people had provided Richard with the contact details of some legal firms who had offered their services pro bono for bushfire victims in need of legal advice.

I remember feeling confused at the 'victim' label being applied to me who had survived, rather than to Barry who appeared to have perished. Richard said that he had already made contact with a solicitor from a firm that operated out of the Melbourne CBD and that the solicitor was investigating what options we might have. When he left to return home, Richard said he would phone me if there was any news. He promised that he would keep fighting to get me Barry's ashes. I did not, for one second, doubt his determination.

Somehow without me realising it, my goal had slipped from finding Barry alive to being allowed to have his ashes. Did I no longer believe that he was alive somewhere? I felt guilty that I had let him down. I sifted through my thoughts. When had I stopped believing that he would come back? I could not pinpoint the time and yet ... here I was talking earnestly about Barry's ashes. I tried to clarify things in my head. Was there some disloyalty in fighting two battles simultaneously? Could I believe Barry would be found while at the same time fight for his ashes? It was illogical. But in holding both ideals at the same time I could live with myself and go on. If I made myself choose between the two I would surely lose my sanity and perish. I could do both. No-one need know. I could do it inside me, where only I existed, where only I would know.

For part of the morning I read through the list of names in the memorial book register. Some handwriting was firm and clear, some in the spidery script of the elderly. The pages were dotted with children's print, perhaps some of Barry's ex-students, and here and there a mother had signed on behalf of an entire family. There were many names that I did not know. There were some surprises: Major Glenys Ford (and her husband) from the Salvation Army, members of the Draft Resisters' Union, the secretary of the Victorian Trades Hall Council, many members of the Australian Education Union and some of my workmates. Showing further disrespect for her brother's wishes, Barry's estranged sister had also signed the memorial book. For what purpose? I wondered. Forever after, there would be her signature, unwanted amidst the others. The list of parents, teachers, ex-students, relations and friends went on and on for pages. People had travelled from Queensland, New South Wales and from across Victoria to attend. Barry would have been overwhelmed to know that so many people had come to pay their respects.

Kayleen stayed with me for a couple of days during which time we were visited by other wellwishers. We attended the theatre one evening, with Kayleen occupying a seat that had been purchased for Barry. During her stay Kayleen asked me if she could have a copy of my eulogy speech. She thought the fairy tale was a beautiful medium by which to have farewelled Barry. She asked me what might happen to the princess in the fairy story now. I gave a shrug. 'You should write the love story of you and Barry,' she said.

I smiled. 'Perhaps in time I might try to do that,' I replied sadly, wondering if I would have the strength.

When I dropped Kayleen at the airport, she pushed a small piece of paper into my hand. It read ... *and the princess flew, with a gentle breeze of distant memory to guide her.*

Later that night I sent an email to a friend. It shows something of how I was feeling.

> *At the moment I feel like I've lost everything ... I'm having trouble just breathing. But everyone keeps telling me I'm doing 'great' and 'it' will all get easier over time. I'm not sure what 'it' is ... but I don't believe them! The fact is ... I don't want to get over it.*
>
> *I've never been so sad.*

Monday 2 March 2009

Richard phoned to ask that I send a copy of the will to the bushfire solicitor. I told Richard that I had not been given a copy of the will and he told me to phone Daniel's solicitor and request one. The bushfire solicitor had said that it was obligatory that any and all beneficiaries receive a copy of the full will.

I rang Daniel's solicitor. He seemed surprised that I did not have a copy of the will and promised to put one in the post immediately. When questioned further, the solicitor said that the will held no instructions regarding the ashes. He said that Daniel was making his decisions based on a list of instructions that Barry had once written and on the basis of conversations held between he and Barry over the years. Trying to conceal my shock at this revelation I thanked him and hung up. I felt that the solicitor's words changed everything.

Later that evening I hand wrote a letter to Daniel's solicitor. I wrote the letter on the princess writing pad that Barry had once bought me. I wanted the solicitor to know that I was not some sort of evil witch.

Tuesday 3 March 2009

I phoned Richard to tell him what Daniel's solicitor had said and then spent most of the day on the internet, researching the role of an executor. The information available about the duties of the executor were thick and onerous to read; however, the general gist seemed to be that the executor was supposed to manage the paperwork about getting money and property transferred to the beneficiaries. I could not find any reference to the 'ashes'.

The police phoned to explain that I would shortly be contacted by a detective from the Phoenix Taskforce who would make arrangements to meet with me to further discuss the information in the statement taken by Detective Cartagena.

I received an email from my sister-in law, Karen. I was grateful that she had taken the time to tell me that my love for Barry was evident to everyone at the memorial service.

> *Dearest Sue,*
>
> *I just wanted to say how in awe we were of you on Wednesday during the memorial service – you were just fantastic. Our heart went out to you, we cried with you, we laughed with you, we were so proud of you – drugs or no drugs – you were up there sharing your heart, your feelings with the group of people some you knew some you did not know. But we all came to understand how you felt about your partner – and we just wanted to say how wonderful we feel about you sharing yourself so bravely with all of us. You did a fabulous job – it was done with love and that shone thru.*
>
> *Sending you all our love – Vic & Kaz*
> XXXXXXXXXXXXXXOOOOOOOOOOOOOOOO

Heath drove me to Waldene late in the afternoon. Despite the notice from the Victoria Police, we were just going to look around briefly and check that everything was as I had last left it. We wandered around the site aimlessly for an hour or so. As dusk approached, I suddenly became fixated with the notion that some government-organised road-clearing machinery would inadvertently smash the small wooded seat that Barry had built for me beside the driveway. He had positioned the seat at the point where I always started labouring on the walk up the steep incline. I could sag onto the seat for a moment and catch my breath.

Miraculously most of the little seat had survived the fire. The thick support on the right underneath had burnt off in line with the ground. The left side support remained intact although badly charred down the length visible above the ground. The top of the seat was hardly damaged; the heart shape that Barry had chiselled into it was still easily recognisable.

Although I knew that I was not supposed to remove anything from the site, I could not stand the thought of somehow losing the seat.

Heath and I did not have any tools with us. I suggested that we could try to dig the 'good' leg out with our hands. Heath did not hesitate. We both knelt down and began scraping and scratching at the blackened soil. The 'good' leg was much longer than I had anticipated. Barry had buried it some 60 centimetres into the ground. When we had dug for about 30 minutes without reaching the bottom of the leg I forlornly suggested to Heath that we give up. I felt sorry for him having to deal with me. The seat mattered greatly to me, but to anyone else it was probably just a charred collection of wood standing in a barren wasteland.

Heath would not be diverted. He continued to dig, his arm disappearing almost up to his shoulder down the hole he was creating around the 'good' leg of the seat. I imagine he was pleased to able to do something to help his mother in all this horror.

Heath laughed about Barry's expert construction skills, commenting that others would have probably only buried the seat 30 centimetres below ground. 'Trust Barry to build a seat like this,' Heath said. 'Remember when he built that deck? He put twice as many posts and bearers in as most people would use. He builds things strong, doesn't he?'

We laughed. It may have been because somehow the seat had brought Barry back here with us for a moment. It may have been because we realised that we would inevitably release the seat from the hole if we just kept digging. We might have laughed because I was a mother in need of help and Heath was the one person at the time able to offer that help. I felt a great surge of love for him. My son had become a man of great sensitivity and compassion.

Eventually Heath managed to dig down to reach the bottom of the 'good' leg and with much heaving and puffing we lifted the injured seat from its deep stronghold. We manoeuvred it into the back seat of the car and brought it to Greensborough, safe from further harm.

Wednesday 4 March 2009

Barry's will arrived from Daniel's solicitor. Barry had completed and lodged it with his solicitor on 23 August 2005. A simple one-page document, it appointed Daniel as executor and listed me as sole beneficiary (with contingencies if I did not survive Barry). A final clause declared no provision in the will for Barry's estranged sister as '… our relationship has irrevocably broken down'.

The will contained nothing regarding Barry's funeral requests. I phoned Daniel's solicitor to enquire on what authority Daniel was insisting that Barry's ashes be scattered. The solicitor advised that he would send some further documentation to me indicating Barry's requests. He said that he would send me a document that had accompanied the will as well as a copy of some handwritten instructions Daniel had from Barry. In addition to the information in these documents, the solicitor reminded me that Daniel was basing his decisions on conversations that he and Barry had shared over the years regarding their respective deaths and funerals.

This all seemed very conflicting to me. I was beginning to feel that I was deliberately only being given part of a jigsaw. I wondered if there was some horrid secret that I had not been privy to and that I was being drip-fed information to protect me.

Thursday 5 March 2009

Thursday's mail brought an eight-page document entitled 'Personal Records', which Barry had lodged with his own solicitor on 31 August 2005 to accompany his will. A letter from Daniel's solicitor stated that Daniel:

> *... has suggested that part of the ashes received from the funeral director will be placed in an urn and given to you to keep and part of the ashes will be placed in another urn which will be scattered in accordance with Barry's written wishes.*
>
> *The ashes that are given to you could be added to the ashes to be scattered at a later date if that is what you wish.*

The thought of Barry separated between two urns was hideous to me. How Daniel could consider this as a dignified end to someone he called a friend escaped me. The suggestion that the ashes could be reunited at some later date beggared belief. The only sense that I could make of this was that Daniel may not have intended scattering his urn of ashes immediately. If that was the case, why not allow me to have all the ashes?

I turned my attention to the 'Personal Records' document. There in Barry's delightfully recognisable handwriting were details regarding his insurance policies, bank details, location of the title to Waldene, superannuation details, health fund information, solicitor holding his will and similar information. Once again I felt pride in Barry's sense and practicality. He was indeed someone to be relied upon; someone who did everything correctly and conscientiously. No wonder I was in love with him.

This document had a section pertaining to his funeral preferences. Here at last I thought I would find Daniel's instructions.

I was confused. Here were the instructions pertaining to his sister Judith and here, too, was the somewhat ironical request that his body be cremated. I knew that he considered money spent on funerals to be wasteful. I could almost imagine his pleasure as he wrote 'CHEAPEST' as his preferred funeral option. But where was the request for his ashes to be scattered?

A separate, single photocopied page contained a mixture of Barry's handwriting and someone else's 'margin notes'. Across the top of the page someone other than Barry had written my contact details. Barry's writing began with the sentence:

Notification of Death to the following. They will be able to pass the word on to other interested parties.

It was so like Barry to describe people as 'other interested parties' if he was thinking about who might be impacted by his death. He was such a solitary being beyond his life with me. He was so self-sufficient, so self-contained. He went about his life being the best, most honest person he could be and assumed that people would not necessarily be interested in whether he lived or died.

My poor darling; I often wished that I could be as certain of myself as you were of yourself. You did not define yourself on the basis of other people's reflections of you, but rather according to your own personal code. It was sufficient for you that you lived up to your own honest code of behaviour.

Following Barry's initial sentence were the names and contact phone numbers of a modest list of twelve people covering relations, educationalists, friends and union officials. In the margins beside this list were hastily scribbled ticks and crosses and notes suggesting they had been contacted, or messages left, or reminders to 'ring back'. These scribblings had obviously been made by Daniel and Sharna as they tried to contact people about Barry after the Black Saturday fires.

Under a subheading 'Funeral arrangement', Barry had written: *No service, cremation, ashes to be sprinkled in Scrubby Creek or from Mount Feathertop. Cheapest possible option.*

Here then at last in Barry's own handwriting was the instruction that Daniel was acting upon. I was gutted.

Below this text under the subheading 'Finances' were listed the reference numbers for Barry's superannuation, investments and his accountant's contact details. A note at the bottom of the page described the safe and the spare keys that could be found at Waldene. Peculiarly, the page ended with the number of Barry's travel insurance policy.

I read and re-read the two documents. Why two documents? Why a formal one with a solicitor and a handwritten one with Daniel? Was this handwritten one to be given precedence over the formal one? Was the handwritten one even legal? There was no signature and no date. Had I not recognised the handwriting and been familiar with the people and items listed there was nothing on the page to even say this document related to Barry Johnston.

The mention of spare keys and the safe made it evident that when writing the handwritten document Barry was imaging a scenario where he died leaving all of Waldene behind, intact. If that had been the case, I would have had many reminders of our love and life together. Barry could never have imagined that fire would take everything from me, including Barry himself.

The mention of travel insurance at the bottom of the handwritten document also suggested that perhaps this was given to Daniel at a time when Barry and I were going overseas together. That too, would make the scattering of ashes more understandable if we died together while holidaying. I reasoned that this document had perhaps been written years ago, even before the formal document lodged with Barry's solicitor in 2005. It may even have been that when lodging the formal document Barry had deliberately dropped the 'scattering of the ashes' from his funeral request in order to leave it up to me to decide what should happen to his ashes.

Years later I pondered the list of people to be contacted. Why was my name missing from the list? Surely I would have been first on the list? What was Barry thinking when he made a list like this without putting my name on it? Maybe he thought I would be with him in the event of his death; maybe the document had been written before he knew me. The phone number for one of the contacts belonged to a house the person had purchased in the late 1990s. The phone number for another person was a workplace they had left years earlier. This document was not recent. I wondered if it predated the formal document that had been lodged with the will in 2005.

I phoned Richard to tell him what I had received and my thoughts on the latest offer about the ashes as well as the differing content in the two documents. Richard said he would discuss the information with the bushfire solicitor.

Monday 9 March 2009

Richard visited. He had been in phone contact with Daniel again. Despite his best efforts he could only report that he was still adamant that he would not give me all of Barry's ashes. Richard had argued with him that there was little difference between giving me half the ashes and giving all the ashes from Daniel's perspective, yet a significant difference from my perspective. Daniel had countered by saying that if he gave me all the ashes, he did not trust me to return them to be scattered at some future date.

Richard queried the definition of 'future' and suggested that I could perhaps have the ashes until my death and that then they could be scattered. At this suggestion, Daniel had ended the conversation abruptly by hanging up on Richard.

It all seemed like some dreadful nightmare. We were squabbling over ashes, when in reality the Coroner had not yet even identified the 'remains' that had been found in the bunker at Waldene as belonging to Barry! It seemed disloyal to Barry and shallow. We had abandoned all hope of finding him alive or of even finding an identifiable corpse around which we could sit and weep for the life lost. Instead we had leapt to focus on nebulous 'remains' to snap and snarl at each other about the ash that may become the final sum of the man; ash, like the soft powder that already drifted in the breeze above the wreckage that once was Waldene.

Richard left to speak with the bushfire solicitor about his latest conversation with Daniel. He was hopeful that the solicitor might have another suggestion or be able to find some loophole that would work to my advantage in securing control of the remains if and when they were identified as Barry.

Tuesday 10 March 2009

Detective Senior Constable Paul Grant from the Phoenix Taskforce phoned to confirm our appointment later that morning. He asked if I could provide him with a photo of Waldene before the fires when he visited. I said that I would make a copy of the photo that I had used on the back of the memorial service cards.

Detective Senior Constable Paul Grant arrived and reviewed the information that I had previously given to police. He was a quiet, kindly man who brought an air of calm with him. He had apparently been allocated a group of specific files relating to people deemed to have been lost in the Black Saturday bushfires. Barry was one of a small collection of people who he was responsible for investigating.

He asked me to elaborate a bit more about Barry's fire preparedness and about the bunker. The typed statement that he later created from this interview described Barry in simple and sincere terms. I appreciated Detective Grant's honest portrayal of our discussion and his inclusion of phrases that showed Barry to be sensible and practical. Detective Grant's statement even included phrases to highlight the love between Barry and I, although such information added little value to the facts pertaining to the fire. I was greatly comforted in the knowledge that the love we had shared was now on record.

Some of the pleasing phrases appearing in Detective Grant's final report included:

> Barry and I formed a relationship that remained strong to the day he died.
> Barry was so talented that ….
> As you can see, Barry was a very talented man… he was very self-sufficient…

Everything Barry did was done with a sense of planning, thoroughness and completed in an orderly fashion.

He was not carefree about the dangers of fire.

I really can't say much more about Barry other than I loved him dearly.

Detective Grant told me that he had been to Waldene soon after the fires went through and that he might be able to answer some of the questions that I might have about what had happened there. He said that a specialist police officer wearing heat protection clothing had arrived at the site on 8 February and located the bunker. Detective Grant was kind enough to suggest that this may have been as a result of the sketch that I had drawn for police at Whittlesea police station. Hearing that I may have been some help to Barry in all this was very comforting to me at the time. However, the final report revealed that the police officer actually arrived at Waldene just after 4 pm on Sunday 8 February. This was about three hours before I had drawn the sketch at the police station.

Apparently the specialist police officer had described the bunker as being partially collapsed and too hot to enter. His report had said that standing beside the bunker was like 'standing next to an open pizza oven'. The police officer had noticed some items inside the bunker and had used a tool of some sort to drag some of these out of the bunker. Other items inside the bunker were beyond his reach. That police officer's job was just to search for signs of life and then move on to the next property. Detective Grant and his team had worked at Waldene between 9 and 12 February, before I was permitted back onto the site.

After an hour or so, Detective Grant ended the interview and left saying that he would be back in contact with me at a later date. I was happy that his visit had provided me with a few more pieces to the jigsaw that I was trying to put together in my mind.

I now knew that I had last spoken to Barry at about 4.30 pm on 7 February and that by late afternoon on 8 February the police had dragged 'remains' from the bunker. I needed to sort out what had happened in that missing 24 hours. I was sure that the more I could piece together all the facts, the more I would be able to make sense of things. Like a child trying to resurrect a much-loved toy from a scrap heap of rags and broken pieces, I needed to sift through the information carefully; un-crumple seemingly insignificant pieces and carefully place each piece, until the overall image became clear.

That evening I received an unexpected phone call from Richard. The bushfire solicitor had told him that I should make an appointment to speak with someone at a funeral parlour. The solicitor said that it was fairly standard practice for the body of a deceased to be released from the Coroner's Office directly to the next of kin. He suggested that if the remains were eventually identified as Barry and if, on the off chance, the typical scenario ensued, it would be expedient to organise for a funeral parlour to be prepared to dispatch a vehicle immediately to collect the remains on behalf of the next of kin.

Acting on the solicitor's advice, Richard had phoned the Coroner's Office to ensure they had my contact details listed as next of kin. The plan was initiated. We were to behave on the idiom of 'possession being nine-tenths of the law'. All we had to do was allow things to progress 'normally' and if we held our breath, did nothing to confuse the system and restrained from showing any glimmer of outward joy, Barry's remains might just be delivered into my waiting arms.

It was such a brilliant plan of subterfuge, smoke and mirrors. We would steal Barry out through the front door of the morgue, in full view of the world and by invitation from the Coroner. Barry would have been delighted to be a participant in this exciting adventure. It was risky but it was possible and it was the best chance we had, given Daniel's resolve to prevent me from ever having the ashes. Here at last was a tiny, almost imperceptible chink in the realm of possibilities.

9

Wednesday 11 March 2009
When the receptionist at the Le Pine funeral parlour in Greensborough arrived to begin her day, the phone was already ringing. After a quick exchange she organised for me to meet with Julie Harwood, their funeral director that morning.

Julie ushered me into the room where I had sat two years earlier to organise my mother's funeral. Little had I realised back then how much that earlier experience would prepare me for this meeting. Julie began to ask me questions in order to fill in the relevant documents. What was Barry's mother's name? What was his first wife's full name? When was he divorced? What date did he marry his second wife? I began to cry. I did not have all this information. The filing cabinet at Waldene that had contained all this legal information had been destroyed. How could I find all the answers in time for me to be able to claim the remains if and when the Coroner identified them as being Barry?

I sobbed out some descriptions of what I had been through since losing Barry. Moved by my story, Julie's eyes filled with tears. She stood up and gently closed the door of our consulting room before returning to sit beside me. I feared that she would insist on lots of paperwork to substantiate my legal standing in relation to Barry, to the will, to Waldene. I was painfully conscious of the tenuous nature of my claim on Barry's remains.

Julie looked at me kindly. 'We can just write "Unknown" if you don't know an answer,' she said softly. I was not sure if she was giving me an 'out' or whether this meant that she would source the information later. A wave of relief rushed through me. Julie pushed a box of tissues towards me, urged me to take a sip of my tea and then we proceeded.

Our conversation turned to the selection of a coffin and flowers and service. I explained that there was to be no service because of the earlier memorial service. I explained that Barry was to be cremated and that no-one but me would come to the funeral parlour to sit with the coffin and that I would come to collect his ashes after the cremation.

It took an enormous effort to explain to Julie that the Coroner had said 'remains' and that I was not sure what that actually meant coffin-wise. Crying openly, I spoke my worst fears – that perhaps there was so small an amount of remains that Barry might only need a child-sized coffin. I hated to hear my words spoken aloud. They hung ashamedly in the air above us. How could such a mountain of a man be reduced to a tiny child-sized coffin?

Julie quickly assured me that legally an adult must be placed into an adult-sized coffin, regardless of what 'remains' the Coroner was working on. I wondered later if this was indeed a fact or was Julie relieving me of my horror of potentially sitting beside a tiny coffin that belied the 'life-sized' person that it was meant to contain. It was a relief to hear her words. Barry would be saved any humiliation and my final vision of him would be that of a large coffin that I would convince myself contained the large, complete man that I loved and remembered.

Julie walked me to the door of the funeral parlour and wished me well. She said she would wait to hear from me and that in the meantime she would investigate any special financial arrangements being made to help cover the funeral costs of bushfire victims. I stepped out into the sunshine emotionally drained, yet relieved that I was a step closer to having Barry returned to me.

Back at home I organised for a bouquet of flowers to be delivered to each of the four girlfriends who had come to stay with me in the days and weeks after the fire. It was difficult to find words that were adequate to thank them for their kindness. The sentiments that I wrote on cards to accompany the flowers fell short of all that I felt inside:

... I knew that if they could just get you to come for me, you'd look after everything ... A true friend ...

I was grateful for your peacefulness beside me and your love all around me ...

Thanks for coming when I needed you and sitting with me as I wept ...

Thanks for catching me when I fell and carrying me when I couldn't walk ...

I went back to work for the first time since the fires that afternoon. I presented a two-hour professional development session to a group of teachers. The school had been expecting me a fortnight earlier, but I had asked for the date to be rescheduled. All the participants were aware of what had happened in my life and that this was my first foray back to work.

I had asked the principal to request that the staff make no comment about my loss or the bushfires while I was with them. I told the principal that I thought I could do the presentation as long as I was permitted to just focus on the professional content of the session.

I took one of the 'memorial service drugs' before I set out for the school. Even so, as I was ushered into the training room I felt my stomach lurch and my hands begin to tremble slightly. The teachers filed in, their empathy evident in the nervous glances they cast towards me.

Throughout the two hours they sat quietly listening to what I had to say and responding when I asked questions. They remained true to the session's focus and never before or since have I had such a polite, respectful group of participants.

When the session ended, almost in a release of tension, the teachers applauded me. A teacher stood up to formally thank me for the presentation and said that she admired my resilience. Her kindness for not mentioning the fires or my loss made me start to sob. I mumbled a thank you and hurried away. I had climbed back up, for the moment at least.

An email sent to a girlfriend that night describes how I coped.

> *... I began by telling them outright that I'd just lost my partner in the bushfires; that this was my first foray back into the world; that I was on drugs and so thought I would be able to do it; that if I started to cry they should just ignore me and talk among themselves and eventually I'd come back on. I said that I had decided to work from the premise that crying in public is less embarrassing than wetting my pants and so I would be OK with tears ... and lastly I asked them please not to ask me how I was feeling/going ... because the answer was 'sh**house'.*
>
> *Having said all that, I went on and did the two hours. A few times the tears welled up. A few times I felt that choking feeling when you think you'll start to cry, and a few times I made inappropriate comments like, 'So if you do this your kids are more likely to understand what a fraction is ... and apparently that's supposed to matter in the scheme of life ... so I'm told anyway.'*
>
> *The teachers clapped me at the end and one made a speech about how she admired my resilience. I wanted to smack her face ... I don't want to be resilient ... I want to be crippled for the rest of my life. I*

> *don't want people to think I'm coping, or dealing with it, or getting over it, or getting on with my life. I'm not doing any of those things ... Barry WAS my life. All I'm doing now is the automatic drivel that people do to make a living while they wait for their life to begin or end.*

Friday 13 March 2009

The Coroner's Office phoned. An email that I sent to a friend later in the day reveals the purpose of the Coroner's phone conversation.

> *The Coroner phoned me to say they don't hold out much hope of being able to formally identify the remains as being Barry so it may come down to my police report and other circumstantial evidence. In any case it seems the remains will be with the Coroner for quite a while yet ... and that's in my favour. Perhaps Daniel will die before they are released!*

Sunday 15 March 2009

Richard phoned. The bushfire solicitor had been in touch to say that he may have found a precedent in a case in NSW some years back. An elderly NSW resident had passed away leaving her two adult children, who also lived in NSW, as shared beneficiaries to her estate. The executor had tried to have the deceased woman buried in Queensland because that was where the executor lived. He argued that it would be more convenient for him that way. The beneficiaries had taken the matter to court to prevent the body going interstate. The bushfire solicitor was investigating what the final judgment had been and whether it might support my case.

This was very exciting news – another possibility offering some hope. It was difficult to determine how much time we might have. At any time the Coroner might decide that they had enough to identify Barry.

At that time they would probably release the remains fairly quickly. The press was daily quoting the number of people still unaccounted for as a result of the fires. The Coroner's Office must have been working around the clock to reduce this number as quickly as possible.

On the other hand, the remains may turn out not to be Barry. In that case, the search would begin all over again and the time remaining would be even more indeterminate. It was like staring down a long tunnel not knowing its length, where it might lead or even if it opened out into the sunshine at some place further ahead.

I went onto the internet and spent a number of hours searching legal sites in a vain effort to see if I could find the case described by the bushfire solicitor. Finally, exhausted and no further advanced in my knowledge, I went to bed, hopeful that tomorrow would bring some good news.

Monday 16 March 2009

Barry's stepbrother, Mark, phoned. He apologised for not yet sending the photo of Waldene that he had promised me when we had spoken at the memorial service. Mark seemed nervous. He spoke of how upset Barry's biological mother had been at the service. He said that the two of them had driven to Waldene and left a bunch of flowers. I remembered noticing a bunch of dying flowers on one of my visits. There was no card with them and I had assumed they had been left by someone who had been unable to attend the memorial service.

Mark's conversation meandered around with seemingly no particular purpose. It was difficult to keep the dialogue going. Then abruptly Mark admitted that there was a problem about getting the photo. I was puzzled. He said that Barry's mother wanted to know if she had been left anything in Barry's will. I felt the blood drain out of my face. Was this yet another situation where the ground would become unstable beneath my tread? Poor Barry; how could someone so wonderful be surrounded by such horrid people?

Stunned, I tightened my grip on the phone receiver. I spoke quietly and directly into the mouthpiece. 'I don't know what Barry left his mother,' I lied. 'Does she want me to pay for the photo? I'll send some money if that's what she wants.' I waited.

Mark stumbled out another apology. 'She says she won't give you a copy unless she's in the will.' I was appalled. So this was the mother who had written in the memorial service guest register: *My loved son, Barry, in my life for 60 years, I miss him terribly. LOVE ALWAYS xxx*

I felt physically sick. I suggested that Barry's mother should phone Daniel if she wanted to know about the will, as he was the executor. I repeated that I had no knowledge of, nor power over anything to do with the will.

Mark hesitated. I am unsure whether he was registering the disgust in my voice or perhaps having uttered his request, he was able to see the horror of it, but for whatever reason, his manner suddenly changed.

'Don't worry,' he said. 'I'll get you a copy of the photo. I've got a key to Mum's unit. Next time she goes to bingo, I'll let myself in, get the photo and take it to have a copy made. I'll get it hung back on the wall before she gets home again. She'll never know it was gone.'

I thanked him profusely. I offered to pay for the copy and all the postage. Mark refused all offers. He said that he would post the photo to me as soon as he could. He added that he would enclose some special medals that he had had made for Barry also. I did not understand what he meant about the medals, but I thanked him most sincerely.

I hung up the phone and burst into tears. I was crying out of sadness for Barry that his mother had given him up for adoption as a baby and had now somehow forsaken him at the end of his life too. I was crying for me, that here was another battle that I should never have had to fight. I was crying out of fear that Mark would not get me the photo. The world was somehow a much uglier place than I had ever have imagined it to be.

Tuesday 17 March 2009
Richard phoned to say that he had heard nothing further from Daniel or the bushfire solicitor. I described the phone conversation with Barry's stepbrother. Richard was as appalled as me. Nothing seemed to be straightforward anymore. Everyone seemed to 'zig' when they were supposed to 'zag'.

In a journal entry headed 'Day 39 today' I had written the following:

> Sometimes these past few days I feel a huge hole in my chest like a lack of air. I feel myself physically trying 'not to fall into the hole'. With very little effort I could just stop breathing and collapse. I miss Barry so much. I can't believe he's not coming back. The tears are only ever just below the surface while I puddle along doing the tedium that is life.

I received an invitation from the Coroner's Office in the mail. The Coroner wanted to explain the processes that they were using in order to identify people who were lost in the fires. Conscious of the distress caused by the time lapse since the fires, the Coroner hoped that explaining the process to the next of kin and providing an opportunity for us to ask questions might be helpful. The briefing would only be offered to the next of kin of the missing people. The group would be kept small and the briefing would take place on

Saturday 28 March in the afternoon at the Coronial Centre in the South Melbourne.

Here then was the address where Barry's 'remains' must be located. I could attend the briefing and know that I was very near to him at last. I could not imagine how close the Coroner might be to identifying Barry. I had told them everything about him. I could not understand why he had not yet been identified. I turned the word 'remains' over in my mind again. What did it mean? I wished the Coroner would just let me look at the 'remains' and I could tell them if it was Barry or not. I knew him. I would recognise him no matter how badly burnt he was. I knew his length and breadth, the width of his brow, the strength of his legs, the splay of his fingers. I knew him!

I rang the Coroner and confirmed my attendance at the briefing. 'No, I will not be bringing anyone with me for support.'

I had become selfish about everything to do with Barry. I wanted to be there for him. I wanted to listen to what was said and not have to discuss it with someone else. I wanted to ask whatever questions I needed to ask without risk of having my words repeated back to me at a later date. I wanted to infer things from the Coroner's words without someone telling me I was wrong to believe that or to hope for that. If I cried, then so be it. I did not want someone consoling me or distracting me, or being upset on my behalf. I just wanted to be me, searching for Barry.

I looked at the letter again. Sadly I realised that the briefing was ten days away. That suggested that the Coroner anticipated that Barry's remains would probably still not have been identified by then. I wondered how long it would take. I had been told it could be 'quite a while'. 'Quite a while' is a totally subjective description. Apparently six weeks was not yet 'quite a while' in Coronial terms.

Thursday 19 March 2009

An email I sent to a colleague reveals a similar sentiment to my last journal entry.

> *I'm in a bit of a dark hole at the moment. I lost my partner in the Kinglake bushfires and I've been on the most awful rollercoaster of police, well-meaning friends, Coroner's office, the press, bureaucracy, solicitors, etc., etc. ever since.*
>
> *I'm (apparently) very lucky because a flock of girlfriends arrived to catch me when I fell. I'm still trying to come to grips with why I was left behind. My partner's remains are still with the Coroner's office and that makes it all the harder to come to terms with everything they keep telling me. They tell me that (unfortunately) I'll survive all this ... Perhaps they're right.*

With hindsight, it seems that the phone call from Mark had been the final straw for me. I had lost my faith in the world. Any hope or optimism that I had been able to find in all the horror of this situation was rapidly being replaced by a sinking state of depression.

Friday 20 March 2009

I returned home from work early in the afternoon to find a message beside the phone in Blake's handwriting. Blake appeared from the kitchen. 'Mum, someone called Michelle from the Coroner's Office phoned to say that the remains have been identified as Barry! They wanted to release them to the funeral parlour. They phoned here because you were listed as Barry's next of kin.'

A wave of mixed emotions swept over me as I listened to Blake speaking. 'I couldn't contact you. You weren't answering your mobile so I phoned Uncle Richard.'

I burst into tears and now, years later I cry even as I write this entry. All the education, all the moral and ethical training, all the family codes of practice, everything I had ever hoped that Blake would learn as my child had come into play in this one pivotal moment. He had taken the call from the Coroner's Office and responded swiftly and perfectly. He had not confused the situation by stumbling in his conversation with Michelle; he had not mentioned Daniel and he had not waited for me to come home. Instead he had risen to the occasion, and in this few moments, had initiated the plan we had so carefully put in place to steal Barry back to be with me at last.

I phoned Richard. After receiving Blake's phone call he had phoned Le Pine funerals in Greensborough and made an appointment for me to complete the final paperwork at their office on Monday morning. Le Pine would collect Barry's remains from the Coroner's Office tomorrow morning.

I could hardly believe it. Barry was almost back with me. I had been waiting for nearly six weeks and tomorrow morning he would be whisked away from the Coroner's Office and travelling towards me. I would actually know for the first time since the fires exactly where he was and he would be travelling towards me. It was wonderful.

The fact that the Coroner's phone call and the organisation with Le Pine had taken place late on a Friday afternoon was somehow significant to me. It was as if Barry was making a frantic rush to be back with me for the weekend. I am forever grateful to Michelle at the Coroner's for phoning as soon as the remains had been identified, rather than waiting until Monday, the start of the working week. In so doing, I felt that she gave me the extraordinary gift of two extra days with Barry.

My original dream of Barry walking out across the bridge at

Humevale, sooty and somewhat angry, had unconsciously shifted to become a focus on a coffin containing his indeterminate 'remains' being loaded into a hearse and delivered to the nearby, familiar funeral parlour. My joy at his return was overwhelming. I awaited the first birdsong of Saturday morning with tremendous excitement. Yet at the same time, deep inside, I held my breath fearing that Daniel might also have received notification that the remains were ready for collection from the Coroner's Office.

Saturday 21 March 2009
I drove to the Le Pine funeral parlour and parked in the empty car park. It was 9 am and I wanted to be there to greet Barry when he arrived. I wanted him to know that I had never stopped looking for him and that at last, today, we would be together again.

It was a warm, sunny morning and I sat thinking about the many clandestine meetings that Barry and I had had in a back street near here many years ago when we first fell in love. We would sit in his car for hours, holding hands and talking. On dark evenings we could see the glass-lit pyramid in the ceiling of the Le Pine chapel. It was somehow ironic that I should find myself sitting here, waiting for him now.

An hour went by and no-one came. I tried to remember if I had ever attended a funeral on a Saturday. Perhaps funeral parlours are not open on weekends, I reasoned. But people die on weekends. Probably Monday is peak time at funeral parlours, I pondered aimlessly to myself as I waited.

I got out of the car to see if there was an 'opening hours' sign on the door of the Le Pine office. It would be slightly tactless if there were one, but nowadays lots of things are handled without sensitivity. There was no sign. I was both relieved and disappointed.

Looking around furtively, I tried the door handle. Maybe someone was inside working.

The door was locked. Totally uncaring of what sort of character I presented by now, I shielded my eyes from the sun and with my face pressed up against the glass door I peered long and hard into the dark interior of the funeral parlour. It remained still and cold, true to the cold bodies that I was sure were housed somewhere in the rooms at the end of the long corridor.

I stepped back from the door to stand and wonder what I should do now. I had definitely been told Le Pine would collect Barry from the Coroner's Office on Saturday morning. It was almost 11 am and no-one had arrived. Perhaps he had arrived here before 9 am and I had missed his arrival.

I went back to sit in my car for a while. The thought that Daniel had collected Barry from the Coroner's Office played at the edges of my mind.

The clock ticked on. Saturday 'morning' was technically almost over. I drove back to the house, quickly scribbled a letter to the manager of Le Pine and returned to push it under the glass door of the funeral parlour. I tried the handle once again. It remained locked.

Sadly I drove back home, there to sit and wait, yet again. I could go neither forwards nor backwards. I sat in silent limbo; a leaf tossed on the waves in the middle of a storm. I had no power and I had run out of ideas. All I could do was to wait for fate to reveal the next hand. The house waited, deathly still around me.

At about five o'clock, the manager of Le Pine Greensborough phoned. He had just found my note. The funeral parlour was closed at the weekend but he had called into the office for some paperwork. He apologised profusely for the mix-up. He said that because the instructions had been for a private cremation Le Pine had not realised that I would want to sit with the coffin before the cremation.

Barry's remains had indeed been collected from the Coroner's Office that morning, but they had been taken directly to the large Le Pine facility at Croydon. Le Pine had organised for the coffin to be stored there until it was to be cremated next week. The ashes would then be returned to the Greensborough office for my collection.

I cried as he spoke. I could not believe that Barry had been driven elsewhere as I sat waiting for his arrival in the car park. The manager apologised again and said that now he understood the situation he would be happy to organise for Barry to be brought to Le Pine in Greensborough on Monday so that I might sit with the coffin for a while. I thanked him and said that I would be most grateful for that opportunity.

I hung up the phone and sat staring into space. So near and yet so far; would we ever be together again, I wondered. This meant that Daniel might still have time to snatch Barry away from me. I had come all this way and yet I still might be denied the chance to be with him again, even for a brief time.

Sunday 22 March 2009

I got the lawn mower out and studied its buttons and levers. I tried hard to remember the ritual that would make the mower fire into life. I tried a few combinations. When I finally figured it out, I spent hours in the hot sun mowing. I mowed the entire yard and both nature strips. I had never mowed the whole lawn before. It took me four hours. Barry used to do it in the space of time that it took me to cook dinner. I finished the task exhausted and uncertain whether to feel proud or sad. I went to bed too tired to decide.

'One more sleep, my love. Tomorrow will find us together again.'

Barry in 2008

Waldene Snowscape (1

First sight of Waldene 2009

The chimney stands sentinel

photo shown to Grief Counsellor

Steps to nowhere

burnt trailer, its
s disintegrated

Replaced cottage,
garden and car 2015

10

Monday 23 March 2009

I arrived early for my 10 am appointment at the Greensborough funeral parlour. I sat in the car park and listened to my breathing, trying to calm myself, trying to be happy, trying to be brave. I eventually left the safety of the car and walked slowly, like some skittish girl on her first date, across the sun-drenched car park to the front door. The door handle moved when pushed this morning. Taking a large gulp of air, I opened the door and stepped into the reception area.

The counter was attended by a woman I had not met before. In a panic I realised that I would have to explain who I was and what I was seeking. I felt my head drop and the sting of tears in my eyes. I stepped nervously to the counter. 'I'm Sue Gunningham. I've come to … My partner, Barry Johnston … I spoke with Julie last week … I …' The tears burst through and I felt myself begin to shake.

The attendant quickly flicked through some papers and said, 'I'll get Julie for you. Would you like a glass of water?' I shook my head, unable to answer. She flew off down the corridor at the same time as a door opened nearby and Julie appeared. She ushered me into the small room where we had previously met. She closed the door behind us. When I was seated, she pushed the box of tissues in my direction and waited quietly for me to regain my composure.

We completed a few more pieces of paperwork and Julie said that Barry would be put into the coffin at the Croydon building and transported to Greensborough during the day. She asked if I would like to come back and sit with the coffin at 4 pm when their last service would be finished. 'You're welcome to sit with the coffin until 5.30 pm when we close for the day.' Her kindness unleashed another bout of crying on my part.

At 4 pm when I opened the door at Le Pine, Julie came towards me. 'He's here,' she smiled, taking me by the hand and leading me down the corridor. She opened a door and led me into a small room. Inside, mounted on a portable stand, was a plain pine coffin bearing one long-stemmed red rose. The only other furniture in the room was a single chair, pulled up beside the coffin.

'I hope you don't mind the rose,' Julie said turning to look at me. 'I just thought you might like it.'

I realised that I had been so intent on just getting here to be with Barry that I had not even thought about this being a funeral parlour and this being a coffin and that naturally there should be flowers. I felt a bit embarrassed.

'I think it's lovely. Thank you,' I said earnestly.

Julie smiled and moved towards the door. 'Just take your time. I'll shut the door and no-one will disturb you. Take as long or as little time as you need. We're not knocking off until 5.30 and you're welcome to stay until then if you like.' With that she stepped out into the corridor, quietly closing the door behind her.

I stood beside the coffin. I mumbled greetings. I felt happiness and sadness and joy and sorrow. I lay my hand on the top of the coffin. Here he was at last. It was wonderful. I stretched my whole arm along the coffin's length. I sat in the seat and gently patted the coffin murmuring 'Never mind love … never mind …' through endless tears. I just wanted to sit there forever and ever. If I could not wind the clock back then I was happy to just stay here, like this, just Barry and me; here in this tiny room.

A soft knocking at the door heralded Julie's return. It was

5.30 pm already. Julie came to stand beside me. 'Barry won't be picked up until tomorrow afternoon. You can come back and sit with him in the morning for a short time if you like. I'll be here from 8.30 am and we won't need to move him from this room until 9 am.' It was so very kind of her to refer to Barry as a person rather than as 'the coffin'. It may be what she was trained to say, but it mattered enormously to me.

I accepted her offer and with great sadness placed my hand on the coffin for one last touch before leaving him for the night. He had returned to me and no-one could ever take away this brief time that we had been given alone; our first since the fires. I shuffled back to my car crying.

I spent most of the night sitting, thinking. It seemed that I might win Barry's ashes after all. But in so doing, had I been distracted from fully concentrating on what I had lost? There was enormous grief in my realisation that this 'victory' was not part of my original plan when I was searching frantically for Barry after the fires. I wept to think that I had been reduced to describing being allowed to sit beside a coffin containing 'remains' as a victory when I had started out hoping that my beautiful, albeit sooty and probably cross, living, breathing Barry would be returned safely to my arms.

Even now, I was anxious that something would go wrong with the big plan. I was worried that Daniel would still somehow manage to snatch Barry's ashes away from me. I hoped to sit with Barry for the half hour tomorrow morning after which I was to fly interstate for a work commitment, returning on Wednesday afternoon. I imagined that Barry's ashes would be ready for me to collect from Le Pine by then.

I sat and I thought. I decided to write a final letter to Barry. I would ask Julie to put it in the coffin tomorrow. Barry and I had always sent each other letters. Love letters, funny letters, postcards; we ran a love story on paper as well as a love story in life.

I wrote a long letter to Barry. I filled the pages with all the things I wanted him to know about what he had meant to me. I tried to write some sort of plan for what might happen in the time between now and when we met again. I tried hard to ease his mind about the fact that he, the stronger one of us, had been taken and me, the weaker one, had been left behind. I wanted him to know that I realised how much he would have hated the struggle that now befell me.

Tuesday 24 March 2009

At 8.30 am I was back at Le Pine to 'hug' Barry's coffin for another half hour. It would be our final time together as 'people'. Somehow the gap between us would change when his body – his 'remains' – were cremated and reduced to ash. Ash was irrevocable. There is no recovery; no medical breakthrough that can resurrect someone from ashes. Beyond ashes Barry and I could only be reunited in the event of my death. When my ashes were mixed with his ashes we would be reunited in the tangible earthbound way and at that time, if one believed in the afterlife, we would find each other. Our souls would fly across the Heavens, and we would be together again.

I gave my letter to Julie, and asked that she put it in the coffin with Barry after I had left. I tried to explain to her about our habit of writing letters to each other. As I spoke I was conscious of her puzzled look. Yet again I felt our relationship held up to the light of 'normal couples' and found to be 'peculiar'.

Julie took me to Barry's room. Today as I sat beside him I felt sadder than ever. This was some sort of 'Goodbye'. When next I spoke to Barry it would be only in my mind. There would no longer be a 'person' as such, only the enormous void where he used to be. I would be relying on that part of Barry that was 'inside' me to reassure me of what he was; what we were. I would not need to search for him in the outside world anymore.

I sat beside the coffin crying and mumbling both to Barry and to myself. At 9 am Julie tapped quietly on the door. She spoke softly and slowly to me. Barry was to be taken to Fawkner Cemetery this afternoon and cremated. I blubbered about the fact that I had to go to work and that I could not be there. Julie reminded me that there was no service being held. Barry's coffin would simply be driven to the crematorium and cremated. On either Thursday or Friday, the ashes would be returned to Le Pine Greensborough. Julie would phone me to organise a time for me to collect them.

I remember staring hard at her face as she explained everything. I held my breath and listened to her words over the beating of my grieving heart. I listened hard, slowly turning over every word, trying to commit the sequence to memory. I felt sluggish. Somehow I had lost Barry but what Julie was telling me meant that I would win his ashes. I wanted to scream. I wanted everyone to know that somehow a terrible mistake had occurred.

I listened hard. I could not decide if the terrible mistake was that I had somehow come to believe that whatever was in the coffin was all that remained of my darling Barry; or that the mistake was that I was here listening to this description of Barry's final demise. I wanted to say something. I wanted to be a final, pleading voice for Barry. But all I could do was cry.

Julie said that Barry would be cremated at about 3.30 pm. In answer to my distraught questioning she said that cremations take just under 30 minutes. Julie asked me for the details of my timetable that day. She listened, and then told me that Barry would be cremated while I was sitting at the airport awaiting departure. I was so grateful that she pegged the time frame down for me. She did it without being asked. She had become accustomed to my need to know where Barry was every moment, ever since the Coroner had released him. I stood with my hand on his coffin for one last time. I tried to send him all the love and longing and sadness that was inside me.

Later, at the airport, I sat watching the clock from 3.30 to 4 pm I was unsure if I wanted the hands to rush forwards or backwards. I was overcome with sadness. I should have gone with him to the crematorium. He would be by himself. What a lonely end for one so greatly loved.

I thought about whether my acceptance that it was Barry in the coffin meant that I had abandoned all belief that he existed somewhere in the world – alive and waiting. Fighting back tears, I watched the clock in the impersonal surrounds of the departure lounge. I could neither halt what was happening nor urge it to be over.

It was almost with relief that I boarded the plane and flew away from everything. I stared out through the plane windows, imagining the slow dance of the smoke from the crematorium mixing with the clouds.

Behind my glazed eyes I could hear my mind screaming.

Thursday 26 March 2009

There was still no word from Le Pine. I was too frightened to phone Julie for fear she would tell me that Daniel had intercepted the ashes before they had left the crematorium. I opted to believe everything would be all right unless Julie from Le Pine phoned me to say otherwise. I could not change anything anyway and so better to cling to thoughts of the positive scenario for as long as possible.

Julie phoned late in the day to tell me that Barry's ashes would be available for collection from Le Pine in Greensborough tomorrow. I was scheduled to be at work at 9 am. Remembering that I had been allowed to sit beside the coffin from 8.30 am I asked if I could collect Barry that early tomorrow. Julie said that would be fine and I hung up the phone barely daring to breathe.

'Almost my love; almost. Just a few hours and we will be together forever.' I did not phone anyone to tell them the news. I was so frightened that something would go wrong even now. Instead I went to bed hoping to bring forward the dawning of the next day.

Friday 27 March 2009
It was now 49 days; seven weeks since Barry had been snatched away from me. I had been trying so hard, for so long to find him and to be allowed to have him back beside me. Now finally it was time. I had brought the two bears, Dekky and Stewie, along for the reunion. We were an excited little collection of three when I parked in the Le Pine car park. Leaving the bears strapped into the passenger seat I hurried across to the front door of the funeral parlour. Trembling with happiness I turned the handle, opened the door and stepped inside.

The girl at the counter looked up. In a hushed voice I said, 'I've come to get Barry Johnston's ashes.' I began to cry. I am not sure if it was the emotion of finally being at the time and place where that simple statement could be said, or perhaps I was still worried that I would be denied them, even at this late moment in time. I pulled a tissue from the box that sat on the counter and tried to calm myself.

'Yes, certainly,' the attendant answered and busied herself with the obligatory paperwork. I imagine I signed some sort of document but I can no longer recall the fact. All my memories of that morning are tied to the image of the attendant handing a pale green paper bag across the counter to me. Inside was a pale green box not unlike a shoe box. Here were Barry's ashes and I was holding them. They were mine! 'Over my dead body,' a phrase my mother used to use, would Barry ever be taken from me again.

Not waiting to check the contents or make eloquent speeches of appreciation, I simply thanked the attendant and turned on my heel to leave. Julie came along the corridor and murmured her pleasure at being able to help. She wished me well.

I positively floated across the car park back to the car. I buckled the bag with its container of ashes into the passenger seat alongside Dekky and Stewie. I felt deliriously, ridiculously happy. I laughed aloud. It was a sunny day and I wished we could all go somewhere for a picnic to celebrate. I resented having to go to work but I was going to take Barry and the bears with me. Just like that; buckled into the car seat.

Sitting there in the car park I sent Judy a phone message. It read:

> *Just picked up BJs ashes. Finders keepers!*

That night I sent an email to another girlfriend:

> *The ashes were returned to Le Pine Greensborough and I picked them up. I buckled him into the front passenger seat and took him to work with me ... and I DON'T CARE HOW CRAZY THAT MAKES ME!!!!! I have waited a long time to have him returned to me.*
>
> *Daniel doesn't know that Barry's remains have even left the Coroner's Office yet. His solicitor and the bushfire one are still locked in discussions to determine the wording of the contract about when/if and for how long I will be allowed to have the ashes. ... I asked*

Barry about it ... He whispered 'Finders keepers, Losers weepers'... and I was never one to argue with Barry. So that's that!

When we arrived home from work for the day I sat the green bag and the bears on a chair in the kitchen while I made my dinner. I chatted happily out loud and somewhere inside my head Barry answered. Then we all sat together on the couch to watch television. A most wonderful feeling of calm and happiness had settled over me. I did not care what the outside world thought about it; Barry and I were together again and somehow that helped right my world.

Later I carefully slipped the pale green box from its bag and pushed it deep under the bed covers along with the bears. I snuggled in between the sheets. I kissed the photo of Barry that I had been crying myself to sleep on every night for weeks. I put my head on his photo, snuggled the teddies to my chest with one hand and lay the other hand gently on the green box. I whispered, 'Good night, darling,' and drifted off to sleep. Barry was back with me, where he belonged.

PART 3

EXAMINED

11

Saturday 28 March 2009
The Coroner held a briefing for next of kin to explain the identification process. I got lost driving to the location and arrived a few minutes late. The building appeared to be deserted except for those attending the briefing.

I was ushered into a large white room where some twenty people of all ages and sizes were seated in a semi-circle, their gaze directed at two women standing out the front of the group. While one woman continued to address the group, the other stepped away and smiling, came over to usher me into a seat and introduce herself. I recognised her name. We had spoken on the phone on a few occasions.

The speaker was restating the reasons why the Coroner had decided to hold this special briefing. I skimmed the surrounding walls wondering if Barry had been somewhere inside this building for all that time before he was released by the Coroner. I thought about how happy I would have been to just sit in my car outside this building and wait, if this was where he had been for all those weeks. I would have been close to him – for my sake or his? I wondered. Just in case he needed me; in case he needed me to speak for him; in case the Coroner wanted to tell me that it was not Barry after all; just in case …

I glanced around the group. Everyone seemed to be clumped together with someone else. I was the only person attending by themselves. I wondered who else among them had already had their lost family member identified and released.

The speaker kept referring to the people they were challenged with identifying as the 'loved ones'. It was a funny term. I thought about it. If the people who were lost in the fire were classified as the 'loved ones' then those of us who were left behind must be the 'unloved ones'. Yes, I could see that it made sense. Surely without Barry to love me I was now 'unloved'. It was an uncomplicated way of describing how the loss of Barry had changed my life. Loved – unloved, sunshine – darkness; I was now the unloved one.

One by one we were asked to introduce ourselves to the group and say where we were from and who we had lost in the fires. I listened with mounting horror as the sad tales unfolded. A husband and wife cried and held each other as they described the loss of their son who had perished along with his friends. The Coroner was having difficulty identifying individuals from the collection of friends' remains. Grandparents who had lost children and grandchildren; a woman who had lost her sister; everyone came from Kinglake or Wallan or Marysville. The sadness in the room was palpable.

When it came my turn to speak, I described how Barry had perished and said how thankful I was that the Coroner had finally identified and released Barry to me that week. I was aware of a disconcerting wave of emotion that swept across the group. People leant forward in their seats. Some shuffled around to look more fully at me, while the slumped body outlines of others visibly straightened.

When the introductions finished I realised that of all the 'loved ones' who were represented by this grieving collection of next of kin, Barry alone had been identified and released by the Coroner. I shrank a little with embarrassment. I understood why my statement of thanks and relief had caused such a reaction from the room.

I looked down at my hands and tried to avoid eye contact with anyone. I wondered if the Coroner had meant to withdraw my invitation to the briefing at the time that they had released Barry's remains. This was an awkward situation.

The Coroner began to explain the process involved in identifying the deceased. She said that three criteria were considered for the purposes of identification. These were: bones, location and circumstances.

She said that under the 'bones' criterion, the Coroner sought to match the loved ones' medical records, dental records and similar physiological characteristics with those of the deceased. The 'location' criterion pertained to evidence that confirmed the expectation by those involved that the missing person would be at the place where the deceased was found.

The third criterion of 'circumstances' required a combination of enough facts and data from the previous two categories and any relevant medical facts and research that convinced the Coroner that the deceased was in all likelihood, the missing 'loved one'.

People asked questions and the Coroner gave honest, simply worded answers. She apologised for the time involved in making the identifications but reminded people of the importance of being sure of the facts before finalising the identification of a deceased person. Some people expressed concern that their missing 'loved one' may never be identified. The Coroner said that her team was doing its utmost to make sure this did not happen and was trying to make the process as fast as possible.

I sat still and silent, hoping to be ignored. I could feel their desperation as they leant forward to ask questions of the Coroner, tears flowing freely down their faces; some unable to get the question out without breaking down. I listened with great sorrow as distraught relations asked if it was necessary to wait for all the remains to be identified if they comprised a tangled collection of a group of people.

I felt so sad for them. Had the meeting been held last week, I would have been one of these grieving people. Having possession of Barry's ashes moved me into a 'lucky' category compared to these poor people. I felt ashamed of my happiness alongside them.

Sunday 29 March 2009
I received a phone call from Barry's stepbrother, Mark. He was very excited and wanted to tell me that he had done what he had promised. A copy of the photo of Waldene that Barry's mother had refused to give me was now on its way to me. He spoke with great happiness and confidence. This was a far cry from his attitude when he had originally phoned at his mother's request for information about the will. Perhaps this was the true measure of the man; that he had risen to the occasion and done the right thing in spite of his mother.

In the afternoon I visited the second-hand shop. I had decided to try to buy a copy of every book that Barry had selected for me to read from the impressive library at Waldene. Before I met Barry my reading had been limited to a few of the classics and lots of poetry, especially Shakespeare. Barry had introduced me to a most wonderful world of reading. He would pile a selection of books in front of me, and make suggestions for what I might want to read. When I had finished the book we would sit for hours talking about it. We were our own little book club. Barry had read every book that was in the Waldene library. He did not keep books that he considered inferior and those books that he enjoyed, he read repeatedly.

I found a handful of the familiar books at the second-hand shop. I specifically wanted the books to be second-hand because that way I could pretend that they were the original ones from Waldene. I began the habit of writing the month of purchase and time elapsed since Black Saturday on the inside flyleaf of each replacement book. I am not sure why I felt the need to do this. Barry was always appalled at people writing on books. I somehow just needed to mark these books as different to any other books that I might be given or purchased. I felt that the writing on the flyleaf was something akin to writing on a headstone.

Monday 30 March 2009
After the briefing with the Coroner's Office on Saturday I kept thinking about just how they had managed to identify Barry from the 'remains'. I phoned the Coroner's Office and asked to speak to the attendant who had seated me at the briefing. When she came to the phone I explained my query relative to the three criteria: bones, location and circumstances.

She retrieved Barry's file and said that the remains were very small; just a few pieces of bone. While this was horrible to hear, it was what I had secretly suspected, based on Detective Grant's earlier statement to me that the first police officer to Waldene after the fire had only been able to drag small pieces of matter from inside the heat of the 'pizza-oven' bunker.

There had been insufficient remains for the Coroner to identify Barry from the bones alone. However, tests done on one piece of bone showed it to be part of a male pelvis. So that meant it 'might' have belonged to Barry.

Another bone fragment was part of the spine up in the neck area. The spurs on the bone were consistent with those that could be expected to appear in a person over the age of 50. Barry was aged 59 at the time of the fires.

The Coroner had been told by police that their records showed that Barry was likely to be found in the bunker. The fact that that was exactly where the 'remains' were located satisfied the Coroner's 'location' requirement.

Finally, she said that the fact that I had spoken to Barry on the landline at Waldene 4.28 pm on the day of the fire according to the phone company's records, placed Barry at Waldene at the correct time.

Upon hearing this last detail I felt a rush of gratitude for the Coroner. She had managed to make me helpful in this whole business. I had not been able to protect or save Barry but at least I had been able to help the Coroner to identify his remains. The things that gave me joy and brought me contentment were becoming smaller and smaller and more irrelevant to the world beyond the fires. My phone call to Waldene had consolidated the circumstances of 'time and location' in Barry's case. I had helped and I was happy for that.

The attendant explained that a formal report would be sent to me in due course. She offered that in the meantime if I had any questions or concerns I should feel free to phone her again. The Coroner's Office had been wonderfully sympathetic throughout this entire ordeal. Some months later I wrote a letter thanking some of the people who presented at an information evening for people affected by the bushfires. Below is a paragraph I wrote about the Coroner's Office.

> *... It was wonderful to hear from 'Michelle' from the Coroner's Office. She answered questions quietly, kindly and with*

> *authority. … she and her whole team filled me with confidence that they were working in my best interests and would do 'more than was required' to meet my needs, no matter how trivial they may have seemed to an outsider. Not only that, they never, ever made me feel that anything they did was too much trouble. The whole Coroner's Office is forever revered in my esteem.*

I hung up the phone and reviewed everything she had said. Here then were some more pieces to the jigsaw puzzle. I was pleased that I knew this extra information, but there were still enormous parts of the overall picture missing. I would keep searching, but for now it was enough to have the ashes and to know that even by itself, that made me 'lucky' by comparison to some.

That night I began sorting through papers and in my computer's hard drive in an effort to find some photos of Barry. The search produced only a handful of photos. I sat crying, hugging the photos and wondering if they would be enough to keep me sane in the time ahead.

Suddenly I had a wonderful idea. Barry had taught at the same primary school for about sixteen years prior to his retirement. That meant that the school would have the annual class photos of Barry and his students. If they gave me a copy of each photo I would have a chronological series of Barry photos almost up until the fires. I quickly and joyfully wrote a letter to the school principal, not trusting myself to be able to explain it on the phone.

12

Wednesday 1 April 2009
Some weeks earlier I had been contacted by one of the many people helping to coordinate support for victims of the Black Saturday bushfire. I was fairly confused for most of the time with regard to who I was dealing with, given that I was responding to requests from solicitors regarding Barry's will, the police, the Coroner, the funeral parlour, the Whittlesea Council, the SES, Centrelink, the Red Cross, the Salvation Army, family and friends and a multitude of other people.

That particular caller had advised me that I was eligible to have a 'caseworker' and that she would allocate one to me if I so desired. I was not sure what a caseworker was and I suggested that I probably therefore did not need one. The caller convinced me that it would relieve a lot of pressure from me if I had a caseworker. Not wanting to offend, I accepted her offer and was told 'someone would contact me in due course'.

David from Nillumbik Community Health service eventually rang to introduce himself as my 'disaster relief caseworker' and we organised to meet at his office at 10 am. His title filled me with dread. 'Disaster' is such a small word for what had happened. 'Relief' suggested that there was some misconception that everything could be fixed or 'relieved' by someone behind a desk in an office. 'Caseworker' made me feel I was a 'case', a case study, a file perhaps complete with a checklist that once worked through would somehow 'fix me'.

I drove to the office building and sat in the car park trying to convince myself to go home rather than keep the appointment. I felt a hundred years old. The office building looked like the office building I had worked in when I had first worked as a clerk many decades ago. How old was 'David' I wondered? Would a 20-year-old be handling my 'case'? What did they want? I wondered.

True to an upbringing that dictated that appointments once made should be kept, I got out of my car and entered the building. A woman came towards me smiling. 'Can I help you?' she asked.

I felt confused. There was no reception area, no appointment ledger. Was I in the right building? I wished myself back into my car and driving away from here. But it was not going to happen. The woman stood watching me for a moment.

'Are you here to see someone?' she offered. 'Do you have an appointment?'

I felt myself slipping away – somewhere deep down inside. I wished I had not come. I could hardly speak. 'David McKenzie,' I mumbled, 'I've come to see David McKenzie. He's my caseworker.'

'Oh, well normally I'd send you upstairs,' she laughed. 'But he's broken his foot, so you'll have to see him downstairs. He's having trouble getting up and down the stairs.'

I looked down at the floor. I hoped that I was fading from view. I said nothing. All my energies were bound up in warding off a sudden rush of tears. I did not care about the broken foot of someone called David whom I had never met. Why did I come here? my mind screamed.

The woman ushered me into a tiny room containing a small table and two hard-backed chairs. A box of tissues stood abandoned on the table. I took the seat farthest from the door as a concession to a broken foot that may have difficulty fitting into the small space. She offered me a glass of water and then hurried away to 'let David know that I had arrived'. I said nothing, wrestling for composure and glad that she had finally left me alone.

I looked through the venetian blinds of the full length window beside me. Outside the sun was shining and cars were driving past. The world did not seem to realise what had happened. I felt like I was in a glass pod, able to see the world but no longer part of it. I sat in silence, staring out through the window; waiting and yet at the same time, hoping that the woman had forgotten about me. I would sit here in the filtered sunshine, neither alive nor dead and I would just listen to myself breathe.

The door opened and a man a little older than Heath entered. He introduced himself as David and apologised for keeping me waiting. David placed a sheaf of papers on the table. Rifling through them he extracted a few and said he just needed to take down some details from me. The interview began. Full name, address, birth date, phone numbers and employment details. I answered quietly and compliantly. David gave me his card and a wad of introductory papers headed 'Victorian Bushfire Case Management Service – Client Service Information Sheet'.

Glancing down at the proffered papers I saw that I was now classified as a 'client', part of some larger group of people who must have something in common and who needed to be 'managed'. I wondered what that might mean. I vaguely heard a door slam on my own decision-making.

Unaware of what I was thinking, David directed my attention to one particular page in my 'welcome pack'. He talked me carefully through the flow diagram that described the grievance policy that applied to the case management service. There was a chain of command and a list of contact details should I not be satisfied with the service provided. It all seemed very important to David so I stared at the page nodding silently as he spoke. I wondered what 'the service provided' was going to be or for what reasons I might have a grievance.

Having completed the paperwork to his satisfaction David sat back in his chair and looked at me. 'So, is there anything I can help you with?' he asked.

I looked back at him blankly. I turned my head to look out through the venetian blinds at the world beyond. A choking sob escaped from my throat and I began to cry. Unable to stem the tears any longer, I buried my face in my handkerchief and cried freely.

Momentarily shocked, David silently pushed the box of tissues towards me. Ashamed, I twisted in my chair to turn away from him. I struggled to stop crying. The sun streamed in through the window searching out my tear-stained face. Beyond the window the world continued.

After a few moments I trusted myself enough to turn back to face David. He looked puzzled. He had probably been trying to work out what had gone wrong so early in this initial meeting. Perhaps he was worrying that I would lodge a grievance against him for something.

I dried my eyes. 'I'm sorry,' I whispered haltingly, 'I don't know what you want. Am I supposed to tell you something … or do I have to fill out a form? I'm not sure what I'm here for. They just told me to come here. I'm not sure who you are or what you want. I'm sorry.'

I had been interviewed by so many people, filled out so many forms, answered questions, stood in queues, been classified and quantified for so long and so many times that I no longer understood the purpose of most or what was required. I had all but surrendered to the system and merely signed where I was told, stood where I was placed and answered what I was asked. I could not work out where David and his case management fitted into the picture. What was he managing? Was this Barry's case or was it me that he was managing? I felt exhausted and stupid and humiliated.

David apologised. He had not realised that I did not know what his role was. He started again. He pulled out another document and talked through the dot points that explained how he might assist and support me. David would meet with me regularly to discuss questions and provide information as it came through about services and resources. He would help me deal with issues about rebuilding and would advocate on my behalf if required.

David asked about Barry and about what happened on 7 February. We talked about what had happened to me since Black Saturday. David was a good listener. He sat quietly as I told my story. His stillness was comforting to me in that tiny room, locked away from the world beyond.

An hour later we finished talking and David made another appointment for me. We met once more at the office and for the next sixteen months, David was a regular visitor at Greensborough and at Waldene. He was a wonderful support and our many conversations ranged from bushfire and rebuilding information to discussions about literature and art and always about Barry.

When my 'case' was finally closed on 17 August 2010, David sent me a letter that closed with: 'Thank you for the privilege of letting me into your life.'

I gave David a parting gift; the book *Ulysses* by Homer. I inscribed the book with a message: 'I hope that this book will remind you of our journey since the bushfires. It too, was difficult and full of challenges. Thank you for helping me through it.'

Friday 3 April 2009
I visited Waldene and was delighted to find that the bridge at the bottom of the hill had finally been repaired. This was the bridge where the SES workers had turned me away that dark night on Monday 9 February when I was searching for Barry. Now once again I was able to drive up to the property from the Whittlesea end of Humevale Road.

Later, back at Greensborough, I received a phone call from Detective Grant of the Phoenix Taskforce. He was ringing to tell me that he had just been advised that the Coroner's Office had identified Barry's remains. He was rather taken aback when I explained that, in fact, Barry's remains had already been returned to me and cremated on 24 March.

I have no idea why there was a delay in this information going to the police but I assume that Daniel was not notified until that day either. I went to sleep wondering if there would be any repercussions from him. I reasoned that it no longer mattered what he did. The ashes were mine and would remain so.

Barry's death certificate arrived in the mail. Large font wording on the envelope warned me that 'the contents may cause distress'. I read the certificate with great sadness. It advised that Johnston, Barry had died on 7 February 2009 at Humevale. His period of residence in Australia was described as 'Life'. I stared at the word. It seemed incongruous in the circumstances.

The 'Cause of Death' was listed as 'Effects of Fire'. I was named as the 'Informant' and 'Domestic Partner' of the deceased. The certificate had been signed and authorised and the death had been allocated a registration number by the Registry of Births, Deaths and Marriages; a one-page document providing a bureaucratic summary of an entire life.

Tuesday 7 April 2009

I sent an email to Richard.

> *Hi Richard,*
>
> *My caseworker, David ... phoned today to see how 'things are going'. He had spoken to the Legal Aid solicitor handling bushfire stuff, regarding Barry's ashes. The Legal Aid solicitor is of the opinion that Daniel is overstepping the mark as executor. (Go figure!!)*
>
> *David said that for my own peace of mind it would be good if we could make it legal that I 'own' the ashes. He wants you, me and he to meet next week to discuss.*
>
> *However, I DON'T want to do anything that might jeopardise me having the ashes. I would prefer to do NOTHING if in some way trying to be 'legal' I risk having to hand Barry over. On the other hand, I'd LOVE to legally own the ashes ... but NOT at the risk of losing them.*
>
> *David asked if you could phone him. I'm HAPPY to do whatever you think is best.*
>
> *Sorry to be a pain ... again, again, again ... I promise to hold the gates of Heaven open for you if you come after I've arrived there.*
>
> *Much love,*
>
> *S xx*

Wednesday 22 April 2009

David visited me at Greensborough. He and Richard had spoken on the phone and agreed that we should talk with the bushfire solicitor about obtaining the legal rights to Barry's ashes.

Richard and I had an appointment with Mr Kelliher, the bushfire solicitor, in the city that afternoon. It was Mr Kelliher's advice that had been instrumental in me securing Barry's ashes.

I was most grateful to him and was looking forward to thanking him in person.

Based on conversations he had had with Richard regarding Daniel's seemingly hostile behaviour towards me, Mr Kelliher had been researching the power of an executor. Richard and I listened in horror as he told us that, legally, the executor has full control over the assets until such time as the final settlement is made. I felt myself physically weaken when he pointed out that, in fact, the law would even allow the executor to sell the land at Humevale without consulting me if he so desired. To all intents and purposes, the executor had complete and independent control of all the assets until settlement.

Richard looked across at me and then put his hand on mine as Mr Kelliher spoke. He must have been as shocked at the potential for this to happen as I was. Already I was panicking that Daniel might just be cruel enough to sell the land, in spite of the fact that some of Barry's remains were still there, interred under the ground in the bunker forever. Richard asked the solicitor what options we had.

Mr Kelliher suggested that as I was the sole beneficiary of the estate, the easiest solution was to ask Daniel to surrender the role of executor and allow me to manage the settlement of the estate myself. I was relieved to hear this simple solution. I hoped Daniel would agree. It would certainly save him any further problems, particularly now that the issue of Barry's remains was no longer in the equation. Mr Kelliher said that he would contact Daniel's solicitor outlining my proposal.

Saturday 25 April 2009
Richard phoned to say that the solicitor had contacted him to say

that Daniel was not prepared to relinquish his role as executor of the will. He said that Barry had designated him as the executor and that he meant to complete the task.

Wednesday 29 April 2009
I sent a letter to Mr Kelliher. The relevant excerpt is below:

> ... *After we left your office I kept turning over in my mind what reason(s) Daniel might have for refusing to relinquish the role of executor. Perhaps he is focused on the payment that executors are entitled to. If that is the case, would you please advise Daniel that I am happy for him to be paid the money, regardless of whether I finalise the will or he does ...*

13

Thursday 30 April 2009

I visited Waldene for a few hours before going to Mernda Primary School, where Barry taught. One of the teachers had phoned in response to my earlier letter and made arrangements for me to go through the school photo albums this afternoon.

I spent three lovely hours moving roofing iron from where it had fallen across the little paved garden we had labelled the 'Moroccan garden'. I got down on my hands and knees and scraped the ash and rubbish off each paving stone, dug out the little frog pond again and raked all the paths around the garden.

That night in an email to a friend I said: 'It makes no difference to anyone and won't help change anything but it gave me great joy and peace to do it ... so I don't care!!!'

At the school I sat on the floor in the corridor beside the bookcase that held all the photos and albums including annual grade photos, staff photos, official yearbooks, school camps, hat parade, footy day, pet day, discos and similar. I was crying continuously at the sight of all the photos of Barry. The staff were enormously kind to me. One by one they found me in the corridor and came to sit beside me, pat my arm and tell me what a wonderful teacher and person Barry had been. I cried all the harder with the realisation of how very pathetic I must have seemed to them at that moment.

I borrowed about 50 photos in all and took them to Officeworks to have copies made. I sat for hours placing the photos chronologically in a special photo album. Here was my darling boy smiling out at me from a time before I knew him, right through until 2004, the year he retired. He grinned back at me as the judge of the Easter bonnet parade, as the lead bush-dancer, as the animal handler at the pet parade, as the cook at the football sausage sizzle, as a guest at a year six graduation lunch and as a gardener at a school working bee.

Saturday 2 May 2009
An email sent to a friend shows how I was feeling.

> *I have an overwhelming desire to just STOP and spend a few months wandering aimlessly around the garden here and at Waldene ... either that or I need to 'run away' and hide somewhere. I feel that I'm being pushed into pretending somehow I've moved on, yet inside I can hardly breathe. It's very hard to explain.*
>
> *It is 84 days today and yet I still cry myself to sleep every night and wish I'd been standing next to him that day.*
> *SG xx*

Sunday 10 May 2009
It was Mother's Day; my first without Barry. I woke up alone and lay in bed with my head buried under the blankets, my forehead resting on the box containing Barry's ashes; the two bears, Dekky and Stewie, snuggled against me. We were a tiny family of odd fellows drowning in grief. Barry had been gone for three months and I felt that I had achieved nothing. There was so much paperwork and so much to be done. I had to keep waiting for other people to repair bridges or to finish their investigations or to give me permission. I wondered if I would ever be given any power over the site at Waldene.

The news reports hinted that rebuilding on the bushfire-affected sites might be delayed until the Royal Commission tabled its final report. I was uncertain what that might mean for me. I did know that if I had to wait too long to rebuild I would probably lose my mind. It was important that I rebuild. I needed to mark the spot where we had lived and loved. I had started mumbling lately that if 'it' all took too long, then I would build a bus shelter at Waldene myself, and I would sit in the bus shelter until 'they' gave me permission to rebuild a cottage.

Heath and Blake arrived for morning tea. Their gift to me for Mother's Day was a circular saw. This was their acknowledgement that they understood my need to begin to rebuild Waldene in some way. They said that they would show me how to use the saw and that I could perhaps begin building small things while I waited for permission to have Waldene rebuilt. Blake admitted that he had been reluctant to buy the saw because he thought I might injure myself using it. Heath had convinced him that I would be able to handle the saw and that in any case, it would only be a matter of time before I would buy one myself.

I was delighted. Little did I realise that this gift proved to be a significant milestone in my life. This was the time from which I would 'swap my silly little-girl buckle-up shoes for work boots'. From now on I would need to almost become more man than woman in order to survive the strain of all the physical work that lay ahead. I would need to become a landscape gardener, a builder, a bricklayer and a stonemason if I was to rebuild and restore the tranquillity that had once been Waldene.

Over the next few weeks I dismantled a small dilapidated cupboard that was in the Greensborough bathroom. Based on my knowledge of sewing, I came up with the idea of using each dismantled piece as a pattern from which I could cut new pieces of wood. I would then assemble the new pieces together to build a replica of the original cupboard. Slowly and carefully I pulled the cupboard apart, labelling each piece and placing it strategically on a large piece of tarpaulin like an enormous jigsaw.

I worked on this project with no prior building knowledge and with no help from anyone. I was very happy in the process. This small, amateur effort was my first trembling step towards the rebuilding of the cottage. If I could build the cupboard, I felt sure that I could eventually build a cottage if I had to. It might not be easy and it might not be perfect, but it could be done.

Thursday 14 May 2009
Richard phoned to say that the solicitor had been in touch to say that Daniel was adamant that he would not allow me to take over the role of the executor. My offer to pay him the executor's fee had not dissuaded him from his original decision.

Monday 25 May 2009
The Coroner's Office phoned to advise that they were about to send me a letter relating to the cause of Barry's death. The police had yet to prepare their final report but this would be available to me on request when it was lodged. The caller advised me that the Coroner's Office could provide me with three free counselling sessions if I needed them or they could organise some counselling in the Greensborough area if I preferred. I thanked the caller but said that I did not feel I needed any counselling at this stage.

Wednesday 27 May 2009
Richard and I had another meeting with the solicitor to finalise some documentation relating to Barry's will and superannuation. Mr Kelliher advised that his pro bono work for me would cease

after this meeting. He was confident that everything had been sorted out satisfactorily on my behalf but added that if I had a query in the future I should email him.

I received the letter from the Coroner's Office. It advised that the Coroner's Office had 'received the cause of death from one of the pathologists at the Victorian Institute of Forensic Medicine indicating that [Barry's] death resulted from 'Effects of Fire'.

I was a bit puzzled by this letter, given I had received the death certificate from the Registrar of Births, Deaths and Marriages more than six weeks ago. I was left wondering just who had identified Barry's remains; the Coroner or the Victorian Institute of Forensic Medicine?

The letter also stated that 'the Government has appointed a Royal Commission to investigate the fires' and that they expected to deliver a final report by the end of 2010. The letter mentioned that as 'a number of fires are the subject of criminal investigations' the Coroner had to wait until all investigations were finished before completing their findings.

Thursday 28 May 2009

When I visited Waldene I was alarmed to find the Grocon team clearing the property next door. Needing the debris cleared from the fire-affected properties both quickly and efficiently, the state government had awarded the contract to Grocon. Being the largest building contractor in the state, Grocon had ready access to an army of workers and machinery. I had been expecting a phone call from someone to organise the date that Grocon would be arriving at Waldene. The fact that the team was next door suggested that they would want to begin clearing at Waldene very soon.

I was distraught. Barry's trailer was still on the property and I wanted desperately to rescue it if it was possible. The trailer had rusted badly since the fires. Its rubber tyres had perished completely leaving two spools of wire lying beside the rusted rims. The rusted tray was tilted drunkenly to one side. A traumatised collection of metal and wire, it was barely a trailer.

But I recognised it with great affection. It was 'filled' with the sound of Barry's voice discussing its dimensions and its price compared to his previous trailer. I could see Barry's grin when he first towed it home to Waldene. I could see him driving it loaded up with timber and sand for each new project. I could see him collecting furniture from stores and taking rubbish to the tip. This trailer was a precious reminder of Barry and of the time back then, before the fire. It was an old friend, a comfort. But now it was at risk.

The notice from the police on 24 February had stated that nothing was to be removed from the site until the 'Coroner's exclusion notice was rescinded' and that the state government would coordinate the clean-up of fire-affected sites. I was not sure what the Coroner's exclusion notice was, but I assumed it meant that I was not allowed to remove the trailer until approval was given. But now I was frightened that somehow Grocon would come onto the site and crush the trailer for removal as scrap metal.

I agonised about what to do. I phoned Grocon and tried to ascertain when they might be coming to Waldene. The man on the phone promised me that Grocon would contact me before they began work on the site. He had no further information.

I phoned Heath for advice. He suggested that if we got some second-hand tyres we could put them onto the trailer and tow it to Greensborough for safekeeping. My Daihatsu Charade was too small to tow the trailer and did not have a tow bar but thankfully Heath's car did. He said he would get the tyres as soon as possible and take me to Waldene in his car.

Saturday 30 May 2009
Heath and I arrived at Waldene at 8.30 am and true to his word, Heath had bought two replacement wheels for the trailer. We struggled together for the next four hours trying to get the two tyres onto the trailer. A few years back Heath had worked for a time as a tyre fitter and was well skilled at the task, but all our efforts were in vain. He was able to put one wheel onto the axle but the second wheel would not fit under the wheel cover of the trailer chassis. We had minimal tools with us and Heath was reduced to using dead branches as a crowbar as he tried to lever the wheel into place. The axle appeared to have buckled during the fire and would no longer allow the tyre to be accommodated in its usual position.

Heath kept trying to bend the axle back into place but without the proper tools it was impossible. I was beginning to doubt that the axle would bend even if we had the use of a crow bar. We decided to abandon the task and return another day after we had thought it through a bit more and collected some appropriate tools.

Sunday 14 June 2009
This time Heath and Blake came to Waldene in Blake's ute. I arrived before them in my car. On the way, I noticed a sign in a paddock that advised that the owner of the property fixed horse floats and trailers. I had passed the sign a million times before but not really registered what it was advertising. Yet here suddenly the word 'trailer' leapt out at me. I sent up a silent wish that we might be able to resurrect the trailer enough for it to be towed to this trailer repair person.

When the boys arrived at Waldene they pushed and pulled

and eventually managed to roll the trailer over so that we could examine its underside. We discovered that the axle was not the problem so much as the leaf spring on one side. The boys worked determinedly, laughing and joking with each other as they toiled. Not once did they falter in their efforts or tell me that the trailer was not worth saving. I felt that had I asked them to fly to Heaven and bring Barry back to me, they would have strapped on mechanical wings and given it their best shot.

After some hours, while Heath strained on a crowbar to create a gap, Blake was able to wedge a piece of metal in between the sliding pieces of a reluctant spring. This proved to be just enough to enable the wheel to be shoved into place on the trailer, albeit in a tenuous attempt at 'normal'. An electrician by trade, Blake produced some wide gaffer tape from the toolkit in his ute and quickly taped the metal wedge firmly into place between the spring parts.

We carefully rolled the trailer over and then stood back to admire the outcome. The trailer was now standing on two tyres. Its drunken slope remained but not as steeply as before. The underside of the trailer was a tangle of gaffer tape and hastily shoved in pieces of metal and wood, all aimed at levering up the collapsed leaf spring. All the electrical cabling had melted in the fires meaning that there were no indicators or stop lights. The injured trailer looked fairly unsafe and totally illegal. We had to get it down the hill, through the Whittlesea township and 3 kilometres further on towards Melbourne, to where the trailer repair person lived.

I was concerned that it was too dangerous. I was worried that we would be stopped by the police. I was terrified that we would have to abandon the whole idea. I waited. I apologised. I mumbled that it probably did not matter if Grocon took the trailer after all. I was speaking to Heath and Blake but I was trying to convince myself.

Heath and Blake reassured me that they could get the trailer to the repair man. They would go in 'stealth mode', Heath grinned at me. This was a word from their childhood. They used to hide in the garden and pretend to be secret agents; spies with a mission to watch unsuspecting neighbours walking their dogs and washing their cars. I was not sure how kindly disposed the police would be to 'stealth mode' if they intercepted us in transit with the gaffer-taped trailer.

We discussed how we would travel. Heath and Blake would tow the trailer in the ute and I would follow behind. We would drive slowly and stay as close to each other as we could to prevent anyone getting in between us. The ute would be responsible for indicating to oncoming traffic and my car travelling behind would be responsible for indicating to traffic coming behind us.

Our biggest concern was that the gaffer tape might tear and some of the metal and wooden wedges would shoot out from the underside, as the springs slammed shut and jammed the trailer suspension again. If a cyclist or pedestrian happened to be in the wrong place at the right time, there could be some serious repercussions. We planned to slow down or even stop, to position pedestrians and cyclists to be in front of the ute rather than beside the trailer whenever possible. It was very much a 'wing and a prayer' scenario.

With clammy palms and a tight grip on the steering wheels, our small convoy drove up the driveway from Waldene and turned onto Humevale Road in the direction of Whittlesea.

As we approached the trailer repair property I gestured out the window for Blake and Heath to pull over to the shoulder of the road. We got out of our cars and stood grinning at each other. We had made it! I could hardly believe that we had managed to do what seemed 'the impossible'. We stood beside the road recounting different parts of the slow drive down from Waldene where we had thought there was going to be trouble. Our relief at making the journey without killing either ourselves or anyone else was obvious. This had truly been a test of our 'stealth mode' prowess.

I asked Heath and Blake to take the trailer up the long driveway to the repair person's house without me. I wanted to sit in my car and wait. I could not bear to hear the repairer say that the trailer was beyond rescue or that it would be cheaper to buy a new trailer. I did not want to see a look of sympathy in his eyes if I tried to explain the situation to him. I had watched in awe as the burnt-out trailer had shuddered slightly before slowly and painfully falling in behind Blake's ute to obediently follow where it was led. I did not want the repair man's prognosis to steal away the happiness I had felt in that moment.

The boys set off. I sat in my car and watched the little trailer jolting wearily along behind the ute. I wished it well and promised it that even if it could not be repaired, I would come and collect it and take it back to Waldene.

It was a warm day. I wound down the car windows and listened to the buzz of the insects in the field grass. The ute and the trailer had turned in behind a thicket and were no longer visible. I waited.

Soon the ute appeared around the edge of the thicket and drove down the driveway. The trailer was no longer attached. My heart leapt into my mouth. Was this a good thing or a bad thing? I had not told the boys that I wanted the trailer back if it could not be repaired. I was frightened that they had left it with the repairer to use for spare parts.

I stepped out of my car and waited for them to park behind me.

Heath spoke first. 'The man said he can repair it but it will cost almost as much to repair as to buy a new one. He said he's fixed a few trailers that were burnt out in the fires. I told him to phone me when it's ready.'

'We told him that you just wanted it fixed – even if it cost the same as buying a new trailer,' Blake continued. 'He'll do the electrical stuff too, so it'll have lights and indicators again.'

I began to cry. It was wonderful news; another small part of Barry returned to me. The boys grinned. 'Don't cry, Ma. You should be happy,' Heath said, patting me gently on the back.

'I am, love. I'm very happy. Thanks to both of you. It means a lot to me.' And with that I could get no further words out. I hugged them both and we stood in the sun for a few minutes until my tears stopped. It had been a long morning but we had made an enormous leap forward.

Wednesday 17 June 2009

Grocon phoned to explain the process for clearing bushfire-affected sites. An appointment was made for me to meet with their site manager, Gordon Moses, up at Waldene next Monday. I hung up the phone sadly. When Grocon cleared the site they would remove all the debris. I would no longer be able to search hopefully beneath the twisted metal, no longer be able to collect fragments of broken china. Everything would be gone. I wondered how I would cope with this loss.

As much as I realised the practicality of removing the debris in order to begin the next phase, at the same time I longed for everything to be left as it was. It seemed that the removal of the debris was yet another 'thing' being taken away from me in the horrible nightmare that I had been enduring since Barry had been taken away from me. I wondered when 'they' would stop taking things from me. What would be left of me when it was all over?

Friday 19 June 2009
Heath phoned me to say the trailer repair person had fixed Barry's trailer. Heath had organised to pick it up after work. It would cost $320 in addition to the $50 that I had already paid for the two second-hand wheels. This made the cost similar to that of a new trailer but I was happy to pay the price.

At 5 pm Heath arrived at the Greensborough house towing the trailer. It was still rusted but it now stood neatly balanced on its two tyres and its indicator lights winked at me as it turned into the driveway.

'The repair man said that it needs to be sanded, and you need to paint it with anti-rust and paint. He also said not to load it up fully anymore because it's not as strong as it used to be,' Heath told me as we walked around the trailer.

'That's all right. I'm not as strong as I used to be since the fires either. We'll make a good pair,' I replied, conscious of the truth in what I had said. I ran my hand over the rusting metal of the trailer walls. It was a beautiful object to me; an old friend returned.

My diary entry for this day shows:

Heath brought the trailer to Greensborough
Barry would be happy!!
xxxxxxxxxxxxxxxxxxxx

That night I slept fitfully because I was worrying that someone would steal the trailer from the front yard where it was parked. There is no garage at the Greensborough house and only limited narrow access to the rear yard. There was no option but to leave the trailer in the front yard.

Saturday 20 June 2009

The next morning I arrived early at the local Bunnings hardware store to buy a strong chain and a padlock for the trailer. I was served by a young man who had been a student at Whittlesea Primary School when I was a teacher there. I had mentored him during lunch-time science club and had taught his older brother. It seemed somehow fitting that an ex-student should help me find the padlock and chain to secure Barry's trailer.

With the trailer securely padlocked to a tree I felt much more at ease. It did not cross my mind that it was unlikely that a thief would risk being caught for attempting to steal a rapidly rusting, small trailer that had obviously seen far better days.

Tuesday 23 June 2009

I replied to a phone message from Joel Masterson, a senior associate from the Victorian Bushfires Royal Commission. Mr Masterson asked me if I would be willing to give evidence at the Royal Commission in relation to 'what happened to Barry on the 7th February 2009'. I agreed, and we arranged a preliminary appointment to discuss things in more detail.

A subsequent letter from Mr Masterton informed me that:

'... If you would like to bring someone with you to the interview for support, you are very welcome to do so. Feel free to bring a relative, friend, caseworker or lawyer. Since we spoke, I have also spoken to Paul Grant and he said that he would send me a copy of your statement within 24 hours. I will forward a copy to you once I receive it.'

My preliminary interview with Mr Masterson was scheduled

for 11 am on 21 July 2009 at 222 Exhibition Street, Melbourne. The government had secured this building temporarily to house the Royal Commission hearings.

Wednesday 24 June 2009
Grocon phoned to say that the site they were working on had taken longer to clear than expected. They would not be at Waldene until Friday 26 June. Timidly I asked if it would be all right if I was at the site while they worked. I felt like a mother taking her child to the dentist for the first time. I just needed to be there in case … in case what? I wondered. In case Waldene needed me? In case something went wrong and I would be on hand to protect this scarred and wounded landscape that held my heart captive?

I was not sure what my reason was. I just knew that I needed to be there; that somehow whatever happened would be softened if I was there to look out for Waldene, for all its memories, for the memory of Barry, for the memory of 'us'. I had given up trying to explain many of my actions. There is no justification in matters of the heart and I was a willing pawn in the game.

14

Thursday 25 June 2009
Already the forest was beginning to return. The growth was ragged and ugly, like the initial regrowth on a patient's skull following chemotherapy. Here and there a moss-like covering began appearing on some of the trees. On closer inspection the 'moss' revealed itself to be small leaves sprouting directly from the tree trunks. Scotch thistles and bracken began to germinate. Seedpods had burst open in the heat of the fire and scattered odd and unfamiliar plants in places they had not previously grown. Blackberries began their insidious spread across unsuspecting terrain.

On a bend at the top of Humevale Road I was shocked to see a burst of lush green against the blackened backdrop. Seemingly overnight a clump of charred tree ferns had exploded into life; a splash of verdant green amidst the charcoal. I pulled the car over to the side of the road to photograph them.

In my photo collection these photos are labelled 'Traitors'. This is an indication of how my mind was operating at the time. I did not want the world to move on. I was horrified that life was stirring in the forest around Waldene. If Barry could not live then I reasoned that perhaps neither should the forest. I wanted this part of the world to just stop; perhaps to be a small shrine to all that was lost. At least it should stop until I could come to grips with what had happened and work out a plan for what should happen next.

But now, here was this burst of colour signifying life; these traitors to the memory of all that had been lost. I felt a sense of urgency wash over me. Time was moving on and I still had no real plan other than the desperate need to rebuild the cottage and therein hopefully restore some sort of equilibrium to my world.

Tuesday 14 July 2009
The trailer rescued from Waldene had now been chained to the fence in Greensborough for over three weeks. It was rusting rapidly because of the effects of fire. Once again I began to fret about how I might save it from this new attack. I searched the internet and phoned a myriad of companies that listed 'rust' in their advertising material. I was searching for something that perhaps was so unique that there may not even be a solution. I felt overwhelmed by my lack of knowledge. I spent hours in confusing telephone conversations with tradesmen about things that I knew little or nothing about.

Each conversation inevitably reduced me to tears as I struggled to explain what I was trying to achieve and why it mattered so much to me. Each piece of information offered progressed me a microscopic step forward in my understanding of what might be needed, what might be possible, and what cost might be involved.

Wednesday 15 July 2009
The mail contained a request from Daniel's solicitor that I sign an accompanying document that would enable the solicitor to begin the transfer of the property title for Waldene into my name. I was relieved to know that very soon the site would be safe from any risk of sale by Daniel. I quickly signed the form and sent it back by return mail.

I had gleaned that in order to most efficiently rid the trailer of rust it needed to be professionally 'sandblasted'. A company in the industrial suburb of Campbellfield, about 15 kilometres from Greensborough, quoted $150 to do the work. This meant that the price of repairing and sandblasting the trailer as well as buying wheels for it was now in excess of $500. This was akin to the cost of a new trailer. But I needed to have this trailer. I was desperate for the resuscitation of this old friend. I organised to deliver the trailer to the workshop on 23 July.

I hung up the phone happy and immediately set my attention to working out how I might get the trailer to the appointment, given my small sedan could not tow a trailer nor did it have a tow bar. Added to this was the fact that I had never previously towed a trailer.

Tuesday 21 July 2009
At 10.30 am I was seated in the foyer of the city building awaiting my preliminary interview with the Victorian Bushfires Royal Commission. People came and went in the foyer and now and then I glanced at their faces trying to discern who, like me, had been affected by the fires and who the public servants were.

I saw a similar question sweep across the eyes of others coming through the doors. Having categorised each other, our eyes dropped to the floor. It was better not to have eye contact. There was too much emotion wrestling inside. I concentrated on being composed. I needed to speak sensibly and remember everything that was important. I wanted the Royal Commission to know all about Barry and about what had happened.

Mr Masterton appeared and introduced himself and a woman who accompanied him. He thanked me for attending and we moved upstairs into an interview room. My memory of this interview is all but lost. I remember fragments of the conversation and I remember crying but whether I said everything that I had considered important or not eludes my memory. I know that I was asked to go through the events of 7 February and that I was asked specifically about the bunker.

In all interviews since the fires my message has remained the same. I have tried to convey that Barry was well prepared for fire and that he was highly intelligent and behaved sensibly in all situations. I was therefore in no doubt that he had behaved sensibly on that fated day also. The fire had been of catastrophic proportions, travelling swiftly in perfect bushfire conditions. As is the nature of a bushfire, it randomly chose to jump some areas and at the same time shoot fireballs into the centre of other unsuspecting spaces. I was not looking to blame or seek retribution from anyone for this act of nature. Barry would have been the first to concede that nature will always claim superiority over man.

I had told the police and perhaps mentioned at this interview that when I first met Barry I had asked why he lived in the forest away from the township. He had told me: 'I don't have to live here. I choose to.' Then he had taken me out into the garden and waving an arm had said, 'Smell the forest, listen to the birds and the creek, look at the sunset over the valley. It's beautiful. Why wouldn't I want to live here?'

According to my diary the interview with Mr Masterson lasted two hours. When we had finished, Mr Masterson said that he would prepare a report for the Commission and that I might be contacted at a later date for further information or be asked to present at the Royal Commission hearing.

On the train back to Greensborough I stared out the window and hoped Barry would be pleased that I had told his story. I also thought about his love of 'privacy'. I remembered him on occasion saying laughingly, 'Tell the bastards nothing, darling,' when he believed people asked invasive questions during interviews or in documents and forms. He had a particular loathing for completing the government census form and had been horrified when I told him that I had once worked as a census collector. What would he think of my telling the Royal Commission about him? I wondered. But it was important that people realised that Barry and the others who had perished, and the CFA who had worked so tirelessly, did not stand a chance against such an immense fire.

When the train pulled in at Greensborough I was still struggling in my mind. Had I done the right thing or should I have remained silent? It was a question I was to ask myself repeatedly in the months ahead.

Wednesday 22 July 2009

Following my conversation with the company that was going to sandblast the trailer, I had remembered that Blake had a tow bar on his ute. I phoned him to ask what might be possible. Blake said that because he drove a company car during the week, he was happy for me to borrow his ute to take the trailer to Campbellfield.

Blake picked me up in his company car after work and drove me to his house. I drove the ute back through the darkened streets to Greensborough. Hunched over the wheel of the unfamiliar car, I drove in the left-hand lane at an orderly 60 kilometres per hour all the way. I was terrified, yet inwardly excited that I had risen to the challenge. I would do my best to do whatever it took. I would keep trying until I could go no further. Fear would not be enough to stop me. If I paid attention to the fear I would be paralysed and that would be an enormous disappointment to me and to Barry.

Thursday 23 July 2009

At 6 am I was in the driveway at Greensborough trying to work out how to attach the trailer to the tow bar. I had not thought about this until now. I knew nothing of how this might be achieved. I phoned Blake several times and he talked me through step by step. I was conscious of time ticking away. I wanted to drive to Campbellfield before there was any traffic on the roads. I hoped to be there by 7 am.

Finally, I drove the ute out of the driveway, and heard the rattle of the rusty little trailer rousing into life behind me. I looked into the rear-view mirror but the trailer was below the line of vision. I caught a glimpse of it in the side-view mirrors as we bumped and bounced along the road and around the first corner. 'Houston, we have lift-off,' I quoted the famous movie line in my head, grinning to myself.

We moved slowly out onto the freeway. Staying in the left lane, I swung my eyes back and forth from the road ahead to the trailer in the side mirrors. Once again I was hunched over the steering wheel, this time my fingers gripping like claws. I could hear myself panting with adrenaline.

I finally turned into the street in Campbellfield. I drove past the factory. It was on the opposite side of the road. This was when I realised that reversing a trailer takes many hours of experience. I tried for a few minutes before deciding to drive on ahead in the hopes of finding somewhere to do a wide arching U-turn. The factories were not open yet and the streets were fairly deserted. I managed to do a U-turn that caused the trailer to groan its way up and across a nature strip momentarily, before bumping down heavily onto the road once more.

I parked and hopped out of the ute. My neck was aching and fingers hurt as they released their grip on the steering wheel. I stretched and walked around to look at the trailer. It stood there small and rusty and patient. I patted a side wall affectionately.

Naivety of what was involved and stubbornness had worked together to achieve a miracle of sorts. We had arrived.

As I stepped into the small, grimy factory office a woman behind the counter looked up. I gave my name and the purpose of my visit before adding with some degree of pride, 'The trailer's outside. I towed it here myself. It was my first time towing.' I beamed. The woman smiled politely and pushed a button to summon one of the men from the workshop.

A tall, loping man appeared. When I explained that I could not reverse the trailer and was just new to even coupling it to the ute the man said that he would bring the ute and trailer into the factory car park and take the trailer through for treatment. I was to sit on a chair in the reception area and wait. I handed him the keys.

Other people came and went while I sat waiting. The reception room was small and ugly. Old posters of car parts and cleaning and polishing products hung sadly around the walls. I wondered what it must be like to be the receptionist working here all day, every day. It was a male-dominated workplace both in its staff and its clients.

I wondered what was happening to the trailer. I hoped they were treating it gently. I had explained the trailer's history on the phone when making the booking and then earlier to the loping man. I did not want them to weaken it any more than it already was. It needed to survive the treatment.

Eventually the loping man appeared around the doorway again. 'It's all done,' he said. I thanked him and stepped up to the counter to pay the receptionist. The loping man hesitated. 'You know to paint the trailer with anti-rust as soon as possible, don't you?' he asked.

'No,' I said. 'Where do I get that?'

The loping man came over to where I was standing. 'You can get it done professionally. We do it here. But we couldn't do it today.

You'd have to bring it back tomorrow. Or you could paint it yourself. It's just that now it's been sandblasted, it'll just start to rust again unless you get some anti-rust onto it quickly.' He spoke quietly.

In my ignorance I had thought that sandblasting would eradicate the rust forever. I struggled to make sense of what he was telling me. 'But I can't come tomorrow. I borrowed the ute.'

The loping man must have seen the panic in my eyes. 'You could paint it yourself tomorrow,' he offered helpfully. 'You just need to put it in the garage tonight. Keep it inside especially if it rains.'

'But I don't have a garage.' My eyes began to sting with tears. 'I don't have a tow bar and I borrowed the ute and I don't have a garage. I don't know what to do.' The words rushed out of me in a crazy plea. I began to cry. I wanted Barry to come and fix everything. I was out of my depth. I could not think rationally. Already the rust was regrouping to attack the tiny ailing trailer. It was all too hard.

The loping man looked at me sadly. He made a decision. 'Take her out back for a cup of tea,' he said to the receptionist. 'I'll be back in a minute.' With that he turned on his heel and disappeared back though the doorway from where he had come.

The receptionist invited me through to another small room beyond the counter. It matched the reception area in ugliness. A small electric jug sat on a cupboard beside a laminated kitchen table and a few chairs. A battered fridge stood exhausted in a corner. The receptionist ushered me into a chair and soon handed me a mug of steaming tea.

After some time, a soft knock on the door heralded the return of the loping man. 'It's all done,' he said. 'We dipped it in the anti-rust mix and dried it off. It's just being put back onto your car again now. All you have to do is paint it. It will be fine. Okay?' He seemed somewhat embarrassed by what he had done; a loping man working in a grimy factory in Campbellfield who had just worked a miracle for a grieving woman who had lost her way.

I smiled and mumbled my thanks. They had been so very kind. I stumbled out an apology for my ignorance, my tears, my panic, my use of their time, for dropping my bundle. The receptionist and the loping man spoke over my apologies, telling me not to worry. We stood up and moved back out to the counter. I asked how much I owed them. The receptionist looked at the loping man.

The loping man shrugged and asked what I had been quoted. I said $150 but that was only for the sandblasting. The loping man and the receptionist exchanged glances. 'Well, $150 then,' the loping man said.

'But what about the anti-rust stuff?' I asked.

'Don't worry about it,' he replied. 'Just make sure you use a metal paint when you paint it. Then you should be right. Take care now.' And with that he stepped back through the doorway and disappeared.

I paid the receptionist and thanked her for her care of me, once again apologising for all my tears. Out in the car park, the trailer looked almost new. All signs of rust were gone and it wore a full coat of pale grey anti-rust paint.

The drive home was spent in quiet contemplation of the number of kind people in the world and the unlikely places that I had found them. I chained the trailer up and returned the ute. The day had been exhausting and amazing. I had learnt a lot about driving and towing and rust and people.

Sunday 26 July 2009

After bringing the trailer home from being sandblasted, I had decided that I wanted to buy a car like Barry's car. I wanted to be able to tow the trailer around to collect items to help me restore the gardens and transport timber to build the cottage or whatever I might have to build myself at Waldene. Having a car that could tow the trailer would enable me to begin the restoration and rebuilding regardless of other people.

I asked Heath to find me a second-hand car for sale that was the same make, model, and colour as Barry's car had been. I wanted it to be dual fuel like Barry's and I wanted it to have a tow bar, just like Barry's. I toyed with the idea of asking the Registration Branch if they would allow me to buy Barry's number plate given that his car had been destroyed in the fire. I had rescued one battered, burnt number plate from the site before Grocon had arrived.

I was trying very hard to bring Barry back in any way that I could. Unable to make progress with rebuilding at Waldene I had become fixated on smaller things, where I still had some control. I painted a plea across the back of the trailer.

My trailer – all I saved from Black Saturday.
Please don't steal it.

Friday 31 July 2009

The mail brought an 'Executor's Statement of Receipts and Expenditure' from Daniel's solicitor detailing what costs had been incurred in the execution of Barry's will. Initially shocked by what I considered to be a very large amount for 'out-of-pocket expenses' and puzzled by an account for $825 from a Ballarat funeral parlour, I decided to write and ask for more information.

Saturday 1 August 2009

My letter to Daniel asked him to itemise the expenses and explain the invoice from a funeral parlour that had played no role in Barry's funeral. I hated this task. I resented having to 'watch my own back' and I resented having my thoughts taken away from Barry and all the turmoil that I was feeling about Waldene.

My anger at Daniel was growing with each encounter. I secretly vowed to myself that when everything about the will was over, I would visit him face to face and tell him what I felt about his treatment of me since losing Barry.

Friday 14 August 2009
A letter arrived from the Coroner's Office seeking consent to release my contact details to the Victorian Bushfire Royal Commission. The Commission had indicated to the Coroner that they wanted to communicate with me. Given that I had already attended a preliminary interview with the Commission, this letter and its attached consent form was puzzling.

The lines of demarcation between the Coroner, the Victorian Institute of Forensic Medicine, and the Victorian Bushfire Royal Commission had become very blurred to me. However, because the Coroner's Office had been so amazingly wonderful to me throughout this ordeal I did not question either their timing or their request. Rather I just signed and returned the consent form immediately.

Later that evening I attended a bushfire community information briefing session held at Plenty Ranges Convention Centre at South Morang. Coordinated by the City of Whittlesea, the agenda included Christine Nixon (Chief Commissioner of Victoria Police) and representatives from the Coroner's Office, the Centre for Grief and Bereavement, and the Department of Human Services.

The room was large and brightly lit. About 60 chairs had been arranged in six rows across the front of the room. Here and there amidst the sea of empty seats, a couple or small group sat hunched in whispered conversations. The entry door was behind the speaker's area, meaning that once seated, it would be impossible to leave without disrupting the presentation. Unsure if I was emotionally strong enough to cope with everything that would be presented, the room layout worried me immediately.

A smiling attendant came to the door to welcome me and ask me to sit anywhere. I sat on a corner seat in the back row reckoning that if I became too upset I could stand and move to the rear of the room without interrupting the presentation. Gradually, as the minutes ticked by, people drifted into the room and sat down. Almost without exception everyone attending was in a pair or small group. I sat alone in the otherwise empty back row. Hoping that the organiser would not ask me to move down towards the front I kept my eyes averted from anyone wearing a name tag.

Christine Nixon, the Chief Commissioner of Victoria Police, was readily identifiable in the room. Before the formal presentations began she moved respectfully along the rows of seats, bending now and then to answer a quietly proffered question or make a comment. She leant on the back of a seat a few rows in front of me and spoke to a couple for a few minutes. When she stood to move away, her eyes caught mine.

I wanted to tell her that I thought the police did a wonderful job during the fires; that I was so grateful that she had organised for so many police to come from interstate to make sure everything was handled properly. I wanted to say how glad I was that some police bent the rules when compassion was needed and that they should not be reprimanded. I wanted to say that I was glad she had foreseen and taken swift action with regard to the likelihood of 'looting' because I would never have thought people capable of such a low act. I wanted to tell her that all the people in the Phoenix Taskforce had been so kind and sensitive during my interviews and I wanted to tell her that just her presence was comforting. She was strong yet kind, powerful yet gentle. I appreciated that she had taken the time to come to talk to a handful of people who were left behind after the fires swept through.

But as I looked up my eyes teared over and I knew that I would be unable to say anything. Ms Nixon must have seen my anguish. Hesitating for a moment, she offered me a small smile and a slight nod of her head before moving away towards the front of the room. I was very grateful to her.

A few minutes before the presentations were due to commence only about half of the seats were occupied. Suddenly a flamboyantly dressed, middle-aged woman wearing high heels and carrying a sheaf of papers arrived and took up a position in the middle of the front row. She turned in her seat and cast a calculating eye over the rest of the audience, who all appeared to be grieving locals who had suffered somehow as a result of the fires.

The organiser opened the evening and introduced the various speakers. When Ms Nixon spoke the flamboyantly dressed woman immediately interrupted her with questions regarding 'her client'. The woman was representing someone from another area, Marysville by memory, who had an issue with how her particular situation had been handled by the police. The flamboyant woman spoke loudly and aggressively. Ms Nixon fended the first few questions.

The woman continued, raising her voice to override others in the room who were trying to ask questions. She made accusations implying that 'people who were traumatised from the horror of the fire deserved … that a sensitive police force should … and what right did the police have to …' Occasionally the flamboyant woman half-turned in her seat and smiled ingratiatingly to the audience as if she somehow thought she was championing our collective cause.

The audience grew quieter. No-one else could say anything because of the domineering attitude of this woman. I could feel myself shrinking. 'Someone get her out,' I mumbled under my breath. My silent curses became angrier: she wasn't even in the fire. She was just a solicitor fighting a case. I began to cry. The couple in front of me were whispering to each other. Their heads were close together and their bodies were sinking lower in their seats. They too were feeling the burden of this horrid woman hijacking the evening for the purpose of some legal victory.

It is to Ms Nixon's great credit that she took control of the situation. Looking directly and unflinchingly at the flamboyant woman, she said, 'This is neither the time nor the place to discuss the case to which you are referring. I am happy to speak to you later at the break or you can contact me at my office, but these people have come to hear about the fires here at Whittlesea and I would be grateful if you would save your speech for after the open forum.' Ms Nixon stopped, her gaze firmly fixed on the woman.

The flamboyant woman turned slightly in her seat. The eyes of the audience no doubt clarified for her that she had made no friends among us. 'Of course,' she mumbled. 'Thank you.' Ms Nixon dropped her gaze and continued her presentation, taking questions from the rest of the audience as they arose. The flamboyantly dressed woman did not speak for the remainder of the evening.

The next day I wrote to the organisers of the meeting, thanking them for their efforts and outlining my appreciation.

Tuesday 18 August 2009

Heath had searched numerous caryards and trawled the internet until he found me a 'duplicate' of Barry's Holden Commodore. I traded my red Daihatsu Charade for 'Barry's car'. Almost without a backward glance at the little car that had sufficed for the past ten years, I slipped behind the steering wheel of the large navy car. The interior was at once familiar and comforting. I was accustomed to being the passenger in Barry's car, but was now willing to be the driver, just for the joy of being back inside 'Barry's car'.

Amazingly the car's number plate had the prefix UBY. 'You buy,' I laughed to Heath. 'That's a message from Barry.' Heath laughed, not realising the truth I felt in the coincidence.

Wonderfully happy, I drove the car out of the caryard and backwards in time. I would park the car in Barry's normal parking space at Waldene. As I wandered around the property I would sneak glimpses of it from the corner of my eye. I would pretend that Barry had just arrived home and I would relive all the happiness that this event had always brought me. I would hear him calling out to me, 'Bunty-bum? Miss Mouse? Mouse-Hauffer? Where are you?' a make-believe game that I would play willingly.

My disturbed state of mind is evidenced in my diary entry for this day which errantly notes 'Barry rang'. I have no idea now who it was that actually phoned me on that happy day.

15

Wednesday 19 August 2009
Having not heard back from Daniel following my request for an itemised account of his 'out-of-pocket expenses', I wrote to his solicitor. I asked the solicitor to follow up my request and asked for an authorised 'Executor's Statement of Receipts and Expenditure' to support the document he had sent to me on 30 July.

Friday 21 August 2009
Daniel's solicitor sent what seemed an extremely terse response to my letter. He advised me that in fact, half of the out-of-pocket expenses related to payment of Barry's credit card. It seemed to me that this was something that it would have been expedient to mention in the original letter.

The solicitor also advised me that 'if you had died before Barry then Daniel would have received a one fifth share of the residue of the estate'. I felt that this was a dreadful statement to write to a widow. In the time since, I have never been able to make sense of why the solicitor felt that this statement in some way justified the executor's out-of-pocket expenses.

Regarding the funeral cost, the solicitor advised that a funeral parlour had been contacted to arrange collection of Barry's remains but as I 'had made alternative arrangements elsewhere [the funeral parlour] were unable to proceed further but were entitled to submit an account for the work done to the date of instructions being withdrawn'. I wondered how a charge of $850 could result from Daniel's completion of a similar form to that which I had originally filled in at Le Pine. A receipt from a funeral parlour in Ballarat was attached.

The solicitor's letter ended by suggesting that the attached summary of out-of-pocket expenses seemed 'fair and reasonable especially given the trauma of Black Saturday and the aftermath of attempting the recovery of Barry's remains, dealing with the Coroner's Court and organising the service'. I wondered at the solicitor's attempt to almost canonise Daniel in his explanation.

I felt a subtle suggestion that I was being repaid for obtaining Barry's ashes. Surely a solicitor's role was merely to provide the itemised list of expenses. I did not need his opinion of Daniel and his actions. I was living the nightmare and trying to deal with some of the added burden he had caused me. My anger grew.

Later when I went through the itemised list I found, among other things, that Daniel had claimed for costs incurred for a weekend he had spent at Mount Hotham in March. The list described this as 'investigating the spreading of the ashes'.

I wished that Barry would come back and deal with all this. Crying, I tried once again to fathom why Barry had chosen him to be his executor.

Wednesday 26 August 2009

A neighbour from Humevale, David Isom, phoned me to tell me that he had wandered along the valley at Humevale on Sunday morning 8 February, the day after Barry had perished. He had taken some photos of various things as he walked along. Within hours of taking the photos he had flown overseas and had not realised until his recent return that Barry had perished in the fires. He said that he had taken a photo of the bunker not realising that Barry had sheltered inside. The bunker was still burning at the time his photo was taken. This meant that his photos were taken before the first police officer had arrived on the scene at Waldene just after 4 pm on the Sunday.

The notes that I scribbled as we spoke on the phone show that David had arrived at his property at about 11 pm on Saturday night. Neighbours had since told him that the temperature had earlier reached 49 degrees Celsius in the valley. David said both sides of Parkers Road were burning as he drove the kilometre from the Humevale Bridge to his place. The stumps of his house were on fire when he arrived and David had crawled underneath with the hose to douse the flames.

He had spent a sleepless night putting out spot fires as they flared around the house and early the next morning, when he was satisfied that the fire had passed through, he had set off to walk up the valley. David said that he remembered Barry saying that he had a bunker and David wanted to check that everything was all right at Waldene. He walked along the creek bed taking photos as he went.

David said that everything was smouldering and he struggled to orientate himself and locate the bunker. When he finally found it, the beams that had held up the roof of the bunker were smouldering and the roof had collapsed. Somewhat apologetically David said, 'I assumed there was nothing in there.' David was anxious that I should have the photos that he had taken in case they would help in some way. He promised to send them through to me the next day.

Hanging up the phone I was thrown into turmoil once again. Here was another piece of the puzzle, but how would I cope with a photo showing the bunker ablaze? The neighbour had walked along the valley as it still smouldered. Why had I failed to do that? Why had I instead sat at the barriers doing what I was told? Could I have dragged my darling's body from the bunker had I been more courageous? Perhaps I might even have saved him. Once again I cursed my cowardice, my adherence to the rules and regulations. Would Barry have done that if the situation were reversed? I doubted it. He would have been wandering, nay running, down the valley to get to me.

I phoned Detective Grant to tell him about this new information. He asked me for David's contact details and said he would follow up. I went to bed trying to prepare myself for what horror the new photos might contain.

Friday 28 August 2009

The photos arrived wrapped inside a single page letter. David had simply written:

> Hi Sue,
> I hope these pics don't upset you too much
> but give a little comfort – if possible.
> Give me a call if you wish to talk anytime.
> All the best
> D

Among the small collection of photos that David had sent me were three that were specifically related to Waldene. One showed the devastation to the cottage. It was similar to others that I had taken myself when I was finally allowed into the property. Interestingly, there appeared to be no sign of flames or even smoke around the tangle of roofing iron and debris even though the photos were taken so soon after the fire had raced through the property.

A second photo was taken a little further up the driveway. The twisted wreck that I had eventually recognised as Barry's car was in the foreground. From this angle, a smoky haze swirled mischievously across the image suggesting that somewhere on the site, the fire was not completely extinguished.

The third photo took my breath away. It had been taken from the top of the ramp that led down into the bunker. The corrugated roofing iron that had served as a lintel over the doorway was clearly visible and intact. The concrete roof above the lintel had collapsed into the cavity beneath that was the bunker. A small flame flickered on the floor of the bunker directly below the lintel.

I stared at the photo for a long time. I grappled with what I was looking at and what it might mean. Later that night as promised in a phone call, I emailed scanned copies of the photos through to Mr Masterson at the Victorian Bushfire Royal Commission and to Detective Grant at the Phoenix Taskforce. David's photo of the bunker was displayed as evidence at the Royal Commission hearing the following Monday.

Monday 31 August 2009

At 4 am I sent an email to a friend.

> *I'm going to the Royal Commission today ... my 'day in court'. Do you think the end of today will find me better or worse? I've been up all night looking at photos of 'before' and 'after' and reading and re-reading diary entries and scribbled, half-crazed messages that I left myself in February ... trying to narrow the times down to minutes and seconds ... trying to work out if I could have done anything better or faster or more sensibly ... anything that would have altered the outcome.*
>
> *I'm pretty sure it was 'all over' before I'd even realised it had started. Game Over!*

I arrived at the Victoria Bushfire Royal Commission just before

1 pm. I had been awake since 3 am turning over all the events of Black Saturday in my mind. There was so much to remember; I was worried that I would forget something important. I did not want to let Barry down.

At 1.15 pm I was sitting in the foyer of the Commission building waiting for Mr Masterson to come and collect me. His office had previously sent me a package of information to explain today's process along with some background information about the Commission hearings.

The Commission was adjourned for lunch. Mr Masterton introduced me to a female colleague and we went into the room where the hearing would take place so they could explain the layout and identify who would be seated in the different sections of the room. Various stakeholders including SP AusNet, the CFA, the state government, the press and other organisations were represented at the multitude of tables lined up across the room. The Commissioners were going to be seated at a higher bench along one wall and I would be called to the witness box beside them. The entire session would be videotaped.

As I looked around the room I felt overwhelmed. The room reeked of legal inference. I was suddenly conscious that most of the people in the room would be focused on finding tit-bits amidst the testimonies that would somehow help them to avoid being held responsible for the deaths and the devastation. It was amazing to me that anyone could think that someone could have halted such a fire. How could anyone be held responsible for such a catastrophic act of nature? I wondered how anything that I said could be of any use to the Commission.

Mr Masterton told me to ignore everyone and everything in the room and just focus on the person asking the questions and on the questions that I was being asked. He pointed out the location of Mr Peter Rozen, the Counsel Assisting, who would be asking most of the questions. His questions would focus mainly on the bunker. I was to take my time and answer the questions in my own words; just the way I had answered Mr Masterson's questions at our previous meeting. The Commissioners might also ask me questions during my testimony.

We left the hearing room to sit in a 'family room' across the foyer. After the lunch break we would be taken to sit at the rear of the hearing room and at 2 pm I would be called to the witness stand. Mr Masterson said that after my testimony I would be returned to the family room and a grief and bereavement counsellor would be available for me to speak with, if required. I was now very nervous but confident that I could tell Barry's story when asked.

I have very little recollection of what I was asked or how I responded during the Royal Commission hearing. I tried hard to just focus on the questions being asked. Later when I was sent a short video clip showing part of my testimony, I saw that I spent most of the time with my eyes lowered, almost speaking to myself. I was crying and struggling to get the words out. I was obviously very distressed throughout the interview but I was pleased to see that although I spoke haltingly, my voice was clear, loud enough to be heard, and that I had answered fully and sensibly on Barry's behalf.

After my testimony, which went for over an hour, the woman who had accompanied Mr Masterson returned with me to the family room and introduced me to a counsellor, Gus Carfi. He had a pleasant face and a gentle demeanour. The woman took a seat and sat silently for the remainder of our time in the room. I was still upset from the hearing and Gus made me a cup of tea before taking a seat opposite me.

Following is an excerpt from my diary about that day:
They sat me with a counsellor (psychologist — Gus) afterwards. I felt small and exhausted. The female solicitor stayed with Gus and me. At one stage when I lifted my eyes from where they were 'worrying' at the edge of the laminex table, I caught sight of her face. She was very flushed and seemed distraught. I think whatever I had said in court was emotional and/or whatever mad ramblings I was doing in the room with her and Gus must have been distressing.

Gus asked me why I'd said in court, 'I'll build something there (at Waldene) — maybe a bus shelter.'

'Tell me about the bus shelter,' he said.

I explained that if I had a bus shelter I could sit in it and wait.

'For what?' he asked (in ignorance).

'I'm not sure ... Maybe for Barry to arrive in a Chariot of Fire to get me.' I smiled.

He didn't know that this original bus shelter idea had started when the Whittlesea Council seemed hell-bent on making it as difficult as possible for me to rebuild on the Waldene site. I had toyed with the idea of just getting a shed built — regulations around these are far less strict at the moment. Then I had thought about how 'closed in' a shed would be.

Given that I wanted to be at Waldene to look out at Barry's beloved 'Land for Wildlife', a shed seemed a stupid construction ... I had figured that perhaps I could get away with a 'bus shelter'. I could go there and sit in it by day and drive back to Greensborough at night. The idea 'pleased' me. It was small and 'mouse-like'. Barry would 'get it' — a bit tragic, but sweet and adorable at the same time. A bus shelter with a girl waiting inside for the one bus that may come past, if she's lucky.

> *Just me sitting and waiting for Barry to come and get me. I would wait and he would find me.*
>
> *I know the psychologist was appalled – but what would he know? What do I care? Barry would understand and that's all that matters ...*
>
> *I feel a thousand years old.*

That evening I received phone calls and emails from friends and relations who had seen a clip of me presenting at the Royal Commission on the evening ABC news program. I had not realised that the press would be allowed to show video footage from the hearing. I wrote a letter to the ABC and asked if they would send me a copy of the news clip.

Jane Cowan, the reporter in the footage, contacted me to say she would organise the DVD to be sent to me. The three-minute news clip included some of my responses and some footage of a representative of the Master Builders Association (MBA) addressing the Royal Commission. The Victorian Premier, John Brumby, also appeared in the clip, making a statement to the press somewhere outdoors. I was shocked to see that David Isom's photo of the burning bunker featured in the footage.

The report began with a voiceover saying, 'Today the Royal Commission heard a distressing account of how a homemade bunker failed to save a man at Humevale.' Following was some footage of me explaining that Barry had constructed a bunker at Waldene and then later crying as I retold my conversation with the police when they had told me there were some 'remains' found in the bunker.

I was interested to hear the MBA representative's testimony. He said that, 'setting minimum building standards to regulate fire bunkers is a difficult prospect. It is difficult to decide what the base minimum would be. Is Black Saturday the base minimum?' His words matched my thoughts. How can you legislate for a catastrophe?

The Premier was filmed declaring that the Victorian government 'will implement everything recommended by the Victorian Bushfire Royal Commission. All 51 recommendations in their interim report will be implemented.'

I thought that was a ridiculous kneejerk reaction to the situation. Also I wondered how he already knew that there were 51 recommendations given that the hearings were still continuing. In any case, surely there needed to be some form of consultation before a government could agree to implement every single recommendation. The fact that the MBA seemed to be struggling with how best to adapt building regulations about bunkers suggested that there was a very good chance that some of the recommendations might work on paper but prove difficult, if not impossible, to put into practice.

The video clip ended with a voiceover saying that 'Sue will rebuild at Humevale where most of her partner's remains still remain'. Sobbing in the witness stand I said, 'I can't let the bush grow over it.'

PART 4

REBUILD

16

Monday 22 June 2009

I met Gordon Moses, the site manager from Grocon. We walked around the site at Waldene and Mr Moses wrote a list of which remaining structures or part structures I wanted to preserve. As I tried to explain why certain parts of the ruin were important to me, the tears flowed freely down my cheeks.

Across the front of the house site was the brick porch that Barry had laid. It was about a metre wide and some 10 metres long. It lay now like a barricade, with the car parking area on one side and the mountain of debris on the other. The location of the porch and the fact that I wanted it retained would present access difficulties for Grocon. I apologised. I began to cry in earnest. I sobbed, 'Barry put every single brick in its place. If I put my hand on any brick it's like I'm putting my hand on top of his. He held every brick.' I could not explain well enough. I did not have the words. All I could do was cry.

Mr Moses wrote on his clipboard. 'It's okay,' he said. 'We can work around the porch. I understand.' He was very kind. He must have had to deal with some awful stories and scenes in his role. I was grateful that he did not complain about what I was asking of him.

I wanted the crumbling ruins of the wine cellar left. 'It was under our bedroom floor at the foot of the bed,' I said, staring at the two broken bottles that were still visible in the mess of melted glass and ash inside the cellar. 'There was a sheepskin rug over the door of the cellar. You pushed the rug away and lifted the door up.' I conjured up a vivid memory of the room as it had been before the fire.

I asked for the three steps that led up from the garden to the pool room to be retained. At the moment they were steps that led to nowhere. I wanted to sit on them and wait for the house to be built out to meet them once again.

The bluestone chimney had withstood the fire and remained standing, although its mortar had dried and crumbled and here and there a stone had loosened or been lost. I asked Mr Moses if it could be left also.

Beyond the house site was the little paved area that had been the centre of the rose garden and another area contained the paving stones that Barry had laid out years ago to replicate a Moroccan garden. 'He could never get anything to grow there successfully. I think the house cast too much shade across it. The soil is not very good either. This little pile used to have a metal sundial on top of it,' I lamented to Mr Moses. I gestured towards a tumbled collection of stones.

The earth here had been so tortured by the fire that it had writhed in pain leaving the ground rippled like sand beneath the waves. The paving stones had shifted haphazardly when the earth had shrunk and moved beneath them. The metal sun dial had melted in the fire and was nowhere to be found.

The bluestone barbecue, though still standing, showed similar wounds to the chimney. Nearby a charred stump from the wooden picnic table still bore one rusted metal bracket. The bracket swung down to the ground now, freed from its task of supporting the tabletop that had perished in the fire; another memory-soaked relic to be added to Mr Moses' list.

We circled back to the secret garden. 'The wrought iron table and chairs were still here after the fire. The chairs were blown over. It looked like we'd left a picnic in a hurry. But it must have been the wind of the fire that blew them over,' I rambled on. The paving stones and wire fence surround of the secret garden were to be kept.

My eyes swept across to the bunker site. It was important that Mr Moses told his team to treat that area with respect. 'That's the bunker. I lost my partner there. The police have filled it in. You can still see the air passage that ran out at the back.' I gestured to Mr Moses.

'Do you think your team could leave the air passage?' It seemed a small, pathetic request even to my own ears and brought with it a torrent of tears. I was not even sure why it was important for the air tunnel to be saved. Perhaps in my mind I was making sure air got into the bunker. Perhaps I was keeping Barry alive. It was too bizarre to think through. I could not explain even to myself. I just knew that I did not want Grocon to fill in the air passage.

Mr Moses wrote on his clipboard. 'You don't have to worry,' he said quietly. 'We will treat this area with great respect and no-one will disturb the air passage.' I cannot imagine what sense Mr Moses was making of my peculiar request but I suppose that it was not the first and would not be the last unusual plea made by the people left behind after the fires. He was well chosen for the task by Grocon.

Mr Moses anticipated the Grocon team would begin clearing the site at Waldene on the Thursday. He promised to phone me if there was a change to that date. After he left, I wandered around Waldene alone. I felt a rising sense of panic. Soon all this roofing iron, all the smashed and melted glass, the rusted bicycle frame, the battered lamps, the broken stove, the bathtub – everything would be taken away. 'They' kept taking things away from me. I was not sure if I would cope. I knew things could not just stay like they were but I also did not want them to be taken away.

I spent some time sifting through the ash again. I tried to lift more of the roofing iron to see if I could find anything beneath. It was impossible. I was not strong enough to lift everything up. I sat on the steps-to-nowhere and wept. It was hard to know what to do. I wished Barry would come back and tell me. I felt very small and very alone.

Friday 26 June 2009

I arrived at Walden just before midday. I was to meet 'Gavin' from Grocon. He would be the key person at Waldene throughout the clearing. I parked my car at the side of the road about 20 metres before the driveway. Already there were workmen's trucks on the shoulder of the road.

I got out of the car and walked to the top of the driveway. New red and white bunting tape had been installed part way down to prevent unlawful entry to the site. Some heavy excavation machines were assembled beyond the bunting. Once again everything was out of my control. I was reduced to the role of observer. I stood looking down at the machinery and the men. I wondered if they knew or cared what all this meant to me. I wondered if they suspected the awful sense of dread that was already pressing down on my chest as I watched them.

Gavin arrived and went through the list of items that were to be retained according to the list written by Mr Moses. He asked if there was anything else that I wanted the team to leave.

The thought of things being taken away from the site upset me terribly. I began to try to tell him how very important it was for me that the brick porch be retained. I began to cry. I apologised for the porch being inconveniently located as far as the excavation work was concerned.

I mumbled that I could not think of anything else except what was on the list. I asked if it would be all right if I sat in my car up on the road as they cleared the site. Gavin said that I could but that there was no need to. All I could manage to say was that I wanted to be there.

That being said, Gavin went off down the driveway towards the machinery and I returned to my car. It was with great sadness that I heard the machinery whirr into action a few moments later. I ushered up a silent prayer that the Grocon team would respect everything that had been written on Mr Moses' list. Down in the valley the cottage screamed out in pain; sounds of suffering as metal and glass and other objects were scraped and dragged around by the huge machinery. Waldene was being raped and I was sitting in my car allowing it to happen.

When the machinery stopped at 3.30 pm I got out of the car and walked to the top of the driveway. Gavin saw me and called up to say I could come down to have a look if I wanted. He was probably proud of what had been achieved.

I walked slowly down the driveway. All the iron roofing had been dragged and lifted over the brick porch and dumped in a pile. I could see the naked ground beneath where the cottage had once stood. It was both horrible and fascinating at the same time. This was the empty canvas upon which Barry had built Waldene so many decades ago. It was surreal.

Gavin ushered me past the machinery and over to the steps-to-nowhere. Here the workers had kindly gathered all the items that they had unearthed and thought that I might want to keep: a collection of rusty cutlery, a small tin of copper coins, a twisted candle-stand. They had been very careful to rescue these mementos that they considered important. Seeing the tiny collection of sad items brought home to me once again how devastating the fires had been. Here were my treasures. These were the things by which I was to remember Barry forever more. I felt overwhelmingly sad.

The Grocon team left and I wandered around the site for a while, trying to reassure myself that this was the right thing to have done. I sat on the steps-to-nowhere and examined the mementos that the workmen had saved for me. I wondered if Barry had ever used the twisted fork or spoon. They might have belonged in the camping gear. I could not recognise them as being from the kitchen drawer.

Gavin had said that the team would not be at Waldene again until Tuesday, because Monday was an RDO (rostered day off) for the building industry. I was glad. I did not think I could have endured the agony of the site being cleaned again so soon after today's horrible experience.

Monday 29 June 2009
I visited Waldene even though there was no work being done at the site. I felt like I was visiting a friend in hospital. I had come to reassure the site that soon everything would be better. I wanted to reassure myself that the brick paving and other items had been saved. I wanted to convince myself that these items had been saved because they would soon be fitted into the rebuilt cottage; they would be the bridge between before and after the fires. They would be a permanent bridge back to Barry.

That afternoon back at Greensborough, Heath arrived to show me how to use the circular saw they had brought me for Mother's Day. His timing was excellent. If I could use the circular saw, I could build the tiny bathroom cupboard that I had dismantled and if I could do that then I could eventually rebuild Waldene. I was anxious to begin. Somehow this would enable me to cover the naked landscape of Waldene following the rape by the well-meaning Grocon team.

Tuesday 30 June 2009
I was back parked on the roadside at Waldene at 7.15 am. It had rained overnight and it was still drizzling. Standing at the top of the driveway looking down, the whole site looked like a muddy mess. The rain trickled down the ruts formed by the excavation machinery; tears upon the clay face of Waldene.

The Grocon team did not arrive until the rain had stopped a couple of hours later. The men nodded nervously to me as they walked passed my car. They were probably as traumatised by the sight of grief-stricken residents as the residents were at the sound of their machinery dragging and crushing the remnants of our lives.

Around mid-morning, two of the supervisors emerged from the driveway and walked along to where I was parked. I opened the window assuming they needed to tell me something. I smiled and held my breath. What was going to be taken from me this time? Had they decided that the brick porch had to go because it was proving an inconvenience?

'How ya going?' one said, leaning down to my window.

'I'm good thanks. Is everything okay?' I could hear the panic in my voice.

'Yeah, no problems. Rain's a nuisance ... slowed us down a bit this mornin'. He glanced up at the grey sky as if checking to see if more rain was on the way.

He looked back at me in the car. 'You know that you don't have to be here. We can give you a call when we've finished. It'd save you having to sit here for hours.' His intentions were kind.

'Sorry. I just need to be here. I don't mind.' The tears began to well up in my eyes. 'I get out and look over the edge every so often. I'm okay. I just need to be here,' I repeated.

'Have you got somethin' to eat?' he asked.

'I've got an apple and a bottle of water, so I'm fine,' I answered his surprising question.

He waved his arm towards the other man beside him. 'We're just going up to the depot at Kinglake. We can bring you back a coffee or something if you like.' I was humbled by these big burly men who swing up into huge machines and toil in rain and sun, with and without amenities or tea rooms or even shelter, other than the cabin in their machines. One would think them to be rough, uncouth, hard and insensitive. Yet here they were – gentle, kind and considerate.

Since the fires I had developed a tendency to try to be invisible, to try to be overlooked, to apologise if I made a problem for people. At the workman's suggestion I quickly mumbled that I would be okay, that the water would be enough. I was overwhelmed by their kindness.

'Okay, love,' he said and they sauntered off down the road to a ute. I looked in my rear-view mirror. My eyes bore the glassy sheen of imminent tears. I looked at my face. It was lined and tired. My fluffy, fly-away hair suggested hasty showers and little combing. I wondered what the two workmen thought of me. I was obviously slightly crazy and very distraught. Perhaps I made them think of how they would like their own mothers treated in this situation and this had elicited the kindness and gentleness they had shown to me.

About an hour later the ute returned. As the workmen walked past my car, one of them knocked on my window. I wound it down.

'There ya go, love,' he said, handing me a polystyrene cup of coffee and a paper bag containing a small cake. 'Can't have ya starving yourself up here.'

I took the warm cup gratefully. 'Thank you. Let me give you some money,' I blurted out, embarrassed by his kindness.

'Nah. We got it up the depot. Don't worry about it,' he grinned. 'Anyway, we'd better get back to work.' And with that they sauntered off down the driveway. I watched them walk away; two unlikely Samaritans, members of the army of kind strangers who would cross my path in the years ahead.

When the work stopped for lunch the supervisor came to tell me that he thought they would finish most of the clearing work that afternoon. They had anticipated bringing the dump bins in tomorrow to load all the debris; however, the bad weather now made this unlikely. The combination of rain, the steep driveway and the amount of debris to be taken away was going to make the task a bit more complicated than usual. The supervisor said that probably no work would be done at the site until Thursday, but that he would phone me tomorrow to tell me what was planned.

17

Thursday 2 July 2009

Two enormous dump bins had been placed part way along the driveway when I arrived at Waldene. The supervisor met me on the roadside and together we walked down towards the house site. He gestured at the bins as we passed them. 'They'll load all the wreckage in those today and take them away. We'll probably be all done by late this arvo.'

I nodded, frightened to look too long at the bins or the nearby mountain of crushed metal and debris that had once been the cottage and everything it contained. I felt that I had forsaken the house that was. I might have made a terrible mistake. We walked on.

'Anyway, thanks for comin' up here this early. I just wanted to show you a problem with the brick porch.' I felt my heart lurch at his words.

No! Please don't take my porch, my mind shrieked. I must have the porch. Please don't take it away from me. Take anything else, but please, not the porch. The silent plea reverberated around inside my head. Outwardly I said nothing. I could not trust myself to say anything. Already I could see myself stretched out across the porch, refusing to move, screaming at onlookers to keep away. I needed the porch. Surely 'they' could not force me to surrender it to their horrid dump bins? I waited for the supervisor to continue.

'The fire burnt the timber that was holding the bricks together. So when we lifted some of the debris, the bricks started to fall away.' By this time we had reached the porch. Along the length of one side, the porch was dug in, level with the land. The parallel side, however, was now about 40 centimetres above the level of the land beyond. This side of the porch had butted against the base board of the original cottage. The 40-centimetre drop had accommodated the original house stumps.

The supervisor pointed out a corner of the porch where a half a dozen bricks had tumbled onto the lower section of ground. 'I can just put another few planks of wood along there to hold it until I get the cottage rebuilt,' I said, dismissing the problem as trivial in the hopes that the supervisor would not suggest that the porch be removed.

I was unsure how I would 'get a few planks' or even secure a few planks to solve the problem but I was certain that I would work out something. I just needed to be left alone with the porch to think it through. All my efforts were focused on downplaying any potential problem with the porch in the supervisor's mind. He seemed satisfied with my suggestion and I breathed a sigh of relief.

The supervisor pointed out the items that had been retained as per my request. The team had done an amazing job clearing away everything but these precious remnants. Yet I was horrified at what Waldene had become. The ground was scraped and cleaned. All signs of life had been removed. No more would I be able to search and scour the landscape seeking artefacts of Barry. I had given Grocon permission to clear the site and now I could never go back to what it was before. This was an unexpected and tortuous end to 'something'. In order to calm myself I tried to reason that this also probably signalled a beginning of something else. But right now, the crushing pain of loss overrode any curiosity about just what this new beginning might mean.

We walked over to the chimney, still standing proudly with its face turned towards the east. Unwittingly, the supervisor dealt me his final blow. 'The council's been up to have a look at how things are going. They reckon the chimney's unsafe, a hazard. They reckon you're gunna have to knock it down.' I gasped for air.

Of course, I thought, knock down the chimney. It survived the fire. It stood and waited until I came back. It watched as all the wreckage was dragged away from around it ... and now, after all that, it too must be destroyed. Why would I think it would turn out any differently?

I stood silently beside the supervisor. I felt myself shrinking. I wished that I could shrink down to become a leaf and just blow away; blow away to somewhere so that I no longer had to watch my life being dismantled piece by piece. I wished that I could go somewhere that I would not be asked to make hard decisions; a place where I was not responsible for 'do-or-die' choices that, once made, could not be unmade. Most of all I wished that Barry would come back.

Recognising my disconnection from his comment, the supervisor spoke. 'Do you want us to knock it over and take it away with the other stuff?' he asked gently as he turned to face me.

'I don't want it taken away.' I began to cry. 'Barry built it with his own hands. He mixed the concrete and pushed each piece of stone into place. I want the stones here with me.' I was crying loudly, unable to get control of myself. This new wound was too cruel.

'We can just knock it down to the point where it's considered safe,' the supervisor said softly. 'We could pile the stones beside it so that you could use them for garden edging or something. How would that be?' He was trying hard to get me the best outcome from the council edict. I nodded assent and thanked him for his kindness.

I wandered back up the driveway leaving the supervisor to manage whatever was to happen next. I was unable to speak anymore. I just wanted to sit in the car alone and be still and silent.

The weight of the dump bins and the steepness of the driveway were proving problematic for the Grocon team. More trucks and men arrived and I felt that my car was presenting a potential hazard. Around noon I drove back to Greensborough leaving the team to finish their work. I was glad that the chimney was still standing when I drove away.

I drove to a site in the suburbs where a builder had small cottages on display. Sadly I wandered from cottage to cottage trying to feel enthusiasm for the task of choosing a replacement cottage for Waldene. Everything looked new, cold and impersonal. Nothing reminded me of the home that Barry had built. I drove away wondering how the chimney was faring.

It is testament to my ignorance at this time that I had not foreseen the mountain of red tape and the new building regulations that would follow the Bushfire Royal Commission. I had thought that all I had to do was choose which cottage I wanted built at Waldene. Had I realised what lay ahead I just might have opted for suicide as some others unfortunately did.

My diary on this day shows a pencilled sketch of a crying face. Beside the sketch is written: 'I hated today!! I'm not coping well – too disorganised, feel overwhelmed today.'

Friday 3 July 2009

When the Grocon trucks tried to navigate the driveway with the loaded dump bins, they became bogged. The bins had to be unloaded in order to free the trucks from their predicament. The bins were then reloaded to half their capacity. The smaller weight enabled the trucks to negotiate the driveway. It was slow and arduous work but eventually the debris was ferried from the site.

The once proud chimney was felled and the team gathered the stones around the base of the small cairn that remained intact.

Saturday 4 July 2009
A letter from Grocon arrived. It said:

> *We advise on behalf of the Victorian Bushfire Reconstruction and Recovery Authority (VBRRA) that the clean up of your property was completed on 4/7/2009 and Grocon control of the property for the purposes of those works ceasesd at that time.*

An attached document notified me that:

> *The Victorian Bushfire Reconstruction and Recovery Authority (VBRRA) has established Site Clean Up Standards, in the document entitled 'The Victorian Bushfire Reconstruction and Recovery Authority: Site Clean Up Standards' (collectively these documents are known as the Standards) ...*

The bureaucratic 'mumbo-jumbo' wording of this document hinted at the sort of language I would find in the mountains of paperwork that would plague all my future attempts to rebuild at Waldene.

18

Sunday 5 July 2009
Perhaps saddened by my visit to the builders display of cottages on Friday, I began to think in earnest about the possibility of building a cottage myself at Waldene. At least that way I could make it more like the original house than the cold impersonal displays I had seen.

But I had never built anything. That was certainly a drawback, I reasoned. I got out the circular saw that the boys had bought me. I re-read the instruction booklet and tried to remember what Heath had shown me during our lesson last week. I was terrified to use the saw. I looked at the bathroom cabinet pieces laid out on the floor. I looked at the pine timber that I had bought in anticipation of building the cupboard anew.

I sat thinking. Nothing would change if I did nothing. I would shrink away; a victim unable to do anything; powerless. I pondered about what was the worst that could happen if I used the circular saw. It was possible that at worst I could sever a limb or cut through the electrical cord and electrocute myself. On the other hand, if I was very careful, I just might succeed in rebuilding the cabinet.

With my heart pumping, I carried the saw outside like one would carry a feral cat; cautiously, slowly, held away from my body. Then after locking a piece of timber in the small workbench that I had bought myself, I pulled on my safety goggles and started the saw. Its deafening roar startled me and I turned it off immediately. I told myself to anticipate the noise and I tried again. It was with something approaching terror that I cut through a piece of pine. Panting with the rush of adrenaline I turned off the saw.

I picked up the timber and examined the cut. I stood grinning.

I had done it. A small step for man, a giant step for me! I wanted to run out into the street and yell out to everyone that I had cut wood using a circular saw. I felt ridiculously happy. I could do it!

I spent the remainder of the day cutting timber. My progress was painfully slow. I cut each piece separately and I turned the saw off after each cut. I was meticulously safe and moved slowly and deliberately. I was proof that 'Rome could not be built in a day' but I did not care. I was using the saw and eventually I would build the cabinet and after that I would build Waldene if I had to. Barry would be proud of me.

Monday 6 July 2009

I was the only visitor at Waldene. With lowered eyes and a sense of sadness I wandered around her scraped nakedness. Sometime later I wrote a poem focused on my feelings about the brick porch.

> *The brick paving;*
> *Before the fire, it proudly led visitors unerringly to the front door*
> *Nowadays – buckled, scarred, rough and irregular,*
> *It sinks beneath the muddy boots of those who trespass;*
> *Tradesmen, police, bureaucrats and the curious*
> *Stomp carelessly along its fragile spine*
> *A failing brick path –*
> *Leading to nowhere.*

Thursday 16 July 2009

I had continued to work on rebuilding the bathroom cabinet. The sound of the circular saw hung over the neighbourhood in Greensborough whenever I could find some time. I finally nailed the piece into place. The new cabinet was similar to its predecessor but much rougher. I had not yet perfected how to overcome my terror of the noise from the saw to ensure that my cuts were accurate. I discussed the problem with a male friend who introduced me to the product 'wood filler'. I bought copious quantities and forced it into the irregular gaps between the gaping joins.

The filler went part of the way to hiding some of the faults. It did not perturb me greatly that the cabinet was far less than perfect. I had set out with no prior knowledge and yet here before me was a recognisable cabinet. I was very pleased with myself, both for what I had achieved and for the potential that this new skill afforded me. In my mind I was already a 'builder'.

An email sent to my brother Richard that night shows what I was feeling:

> *I'm doing 'good' here. I've been practising using my circular saw. I built a little cupboard for the bathroom ... it's not magnificent (except to me). I call it an example of Depression woodwork, not unlike Depression glassware. Double entendre – great with words aren't I?*

Saturday 18 July 2009

I visited a rebuilding expo at Lilydale. I had received the brochure about the expo in some literature from the VBRRA. It promised to showcase cutting-edge innovations for people rebuilding after the bushfires. I went hoping to find a cottage that I might have built at Waldene.

The expo was crowded with people and all manner of exhibitors were present. While some stalls offered draughtsman and architects and new innovative building materials, others related to water tanks, barns, wildlife, charity and food. The whole place had a rural showgrounds feel, with many people apparently wandering around as a form of entertainment rather than seeking rebuilding advice. The crowd surged up and down narrow aisles between stalls and flowed out around the food and drinking area beyond.

I felt myself shrinking. I was unsure where to start. I stopped beside a stall selling Quaker barns. I was trying to imagine if such a barn with a mezzanine sleeping loft might be a good idea for Waldene. It would be built of timber like the original cottage and would give the appearance of a second storey, which would go some way to replacing the view from the vantage point of the 'Indian' bedroom that Barry had added as a second storey at Waldene some ten years ago.

A young salesman approached me. 'So, madam, what can I help you with today? Are you interested in our barns?' he grinned.

I searched frantically for words. I would have to explain everything to him. I looked at the glossy posters on the display board behind him. 'Can people have these as a house?' I asked quietly. He looked momentarily puzzled as he handed me a small advertising brochure and began his sales pitch. 'Well, we could easily modify them to become a house. They are barns, but if we lined them and sorted out some internal walls, they could make a cosy little holiday house. Are you looking for a holiday house?' he asked, unaware of the great sadness that washed over me at the sound of his words.

A 'barn', a 'holiday' house; how could these be a replacement for all that had been lost? The young man waited for my response. I felt my chest tighten and the tears begin to sting behind my eyes. 'I want to rebuild a house that was destroyed in the fires,' I whispered, dropping my eyes in the hopes he would not ask anything more.

'I'm sorry,' he said. 'Did you lose everything?' It was the beginning of a question stream to which I had become familiar.

I wished that he would stop talking. I wished that I would shrink away to nothing and not have to reply. I wished that I had a different answer.

'Yes,' I mumbled hurrying to divert his thoughts by quickly asking, 'Is the frame wood or metal?' I did not listen to his answer but instead, part way through his spiel, I nodded my thanks and moved away, seeming to study his brochure as I went.

I stood staring at some architect's designs for granny flats. They were small but some boasted two bedrooms. This seemed ample for my needs. The artist's impressions showed them surrounded by flowers and trees. As I watched a virtual house tour on a small television screen a middle-aged saleswoman approached me.

Was I looking for a granny flat for myself or for a relation? I was trapped between the television and some large billboards bearing the designs. 'For myself,' I whispered.

'What suburb will you be building in?' she asked. I knew what was coming. I looked around frantically seeking an escape route without being rude to the woman.

'Humevale, near Kinglake. I'm replacing a house that was destroyed in the fires.' I rushed the words out and looked away. The woman looked hard at me. Something in my face or voice had alarmed her.

'I'm sorry,' she said. At this I began to sob. I wondered if the world was 'sorry'. I wished they would stop telling me that. It did not help me. I was drowning in my own sorrow and adding their sorrow to the burden was too much for me to bear.

The woman reached out and patted my back. 'Why don't you sit down on this chair for a minute,' she suggested, at the same time pushing me gently into a collapsible seat behind the main billboard. 'I'll get you a glass of water and you can just sit there quietly until you feel a bit better,' she murmured.

Unable to speak, I nodded my tear-streaked face at her. I sat, staring down at my shoes, trying to make my mind fly up and away to think of other places, other things; anything but here and now.

The woman returned and handed me a glass of water. She patted my back a few times and said that she would leave me alone. With that she turned and moved to the front of her stall to hand out brochures and shepherd people away from the hidden area where I was sitting trying to regain control of my tears.

I realised that coming to the expo had not been a good idea. I was not yet strong enough to engage in any sort of reasonable discussion about Waldene. I would have a cup of coffee and return to Greensborough. There would be time for architects and designs at some time in the future.

Standing up, I sought out the saleswoman, to thank her and return her glass. She wished me well and once again patted me on the back. I moved out into the crowd, to be jostled along to the food court. Around me, everyone seemed to be part of a pair or a group. I seemed the solitary singular oddity in a sea of happy families. Sadness settled down across my shoulders.

Before going to order my coffee I wandered over to a stall offering people information about native wildlife and native plants. I glanced at their brochures thinking vaguely that I could perhaps begin planting something in the charred flowerbeds at Waldene while I waited to work out the rebuilding plan. A woman pushed passed me to ask the man behind the stall a question. I took a step back to allow her passage. At the same moment an enormous gust of wind whistled through the marquee tumbling some of the brochures off the table and onto the ground below. I bent to gather the fallen brochures and a billboard came crashing down across my wrist.

The pain was sharp. I lifted the billboard up to examine the damage. My wrist was bleeding and the skin around was already bruising. The beautiful silver bracelet that Barry had bought me fifteen years earlier had been broken by the corner of the billboard. The sight of the broken bracelet tore through my heart. I had stepped back exactly the right amount for the corner of the billboard to fall right across the bracelet. One minute earlier, one metre further, any other part of my body would have gladly borne the brunt of the billboard. But no, the narrow width of the bracelet had been sliced like a body beneath a guillotine. Surely the blood flowing from the wound was coming directly from my heart. How could life be so cruel?

I lifted the broken chain from the ground and slipped it into my pocket. I dabbed at my bleeding wrist with the tear-stained handkerchief. I pushed the billboard back into place as others collected the fallen brochures. I was glad that no-one had noticed that I had been injured. The hum of conversations had resumed in the marquee.

Avoiding eye contact with anyone, I walked quickly to my car. Sitting there in the car park I examined the broken chain and wept torrents. I felt very much alone and overwhelmed with sadness. Was today some sort of message from Barry? The odds of the freak gust of wind dealing me such a terrible blow were unbelievable.

I drove home struggling to understand what Barry's message might be. Did he want me to abandon my dream of rebuilding at Waldene? Was he trying to tell me to abandon the past completely and forget him? Surely not; he would know that I would never do that. He also knew that I was stubborn when I set my mind on something. Perhaps it was some sort of test of my resolve. Maybe it was just bad luck that I was standing in the wrong place at the wrong time, I reasoned with myself.

Saturday 1 August 2009
My caseworker, David, had provided me with some advertising material about a company that was producing small cottages for people who had lost their homes in the bushfires. They were economical and fast to construct, being comprised of multiple panel pieces that fitted together into a rectangular series of pods. Today I was to meet a company representative and view one of the 'pods' on site at Kinglake.

The 'pod' turned out to be more like a small caravan without wheels. The relocatable structure featured Colorbond corrugated external walls and a semi-curved Colorbond corrugated roof. The structure was mounted on small concrete blocks placed on a level bed of gravel. It reminded me of the Nissan huts that my parents had lived in following World War II when building materials were in short supply.

The representative estimated that it would cost me about $39 000 to purchase the smallest pod, which at 3.7 metres by 8.7 metres was about 33 metres squared. This cost included purchase of the basic pod and construction. There would be additional cost for internal walls, painting, plumbing and fixtures. At a rough estimate I would be looking at about $60 000–$65 000. While I was very anxious to rebuild, this seemed a lot of money for a depressing corrugated hut that had a 'temporary' feel about it. I doubted that Barry would feel that a pod was a worthwhile shrine to the memory of the original Waldene cottage. I was sure that I would be disappointed in myself if I chose this option.

I thanked the representative saying I would think about it

further and be in touch. He informed me that the 'pod' could be constructed on site within ten days if I decided to go ahead. This time frame provided some temptation, but one more glance at the sad little structure convinced me that I could wait a bit longer.

Wednesday 5 August 2009

I was anxious to begin rebuilding at Waldene but I lacked any knowledge of what steps were involved. I had phoned the Building Department at Whittlesea Council the previous week and after lots of crying and confused questions by me and complicated answers from them, I had succeeded in organising a meeting between relevant council people and me, on site at Waldene.

I took a new notebook and pens and arrived early, determined to obtain clarification from each council person about what they required from me.

At 10 am a small convoy of council cars pulled up on the road and an assembly of men spilled out onto the verge. I watched them from the brick porch as they shuffled down the steep driveway. They introduced themselves: a building inspector, a person responsible for the council's water, sewerage and septic issues, some men from the land management and sustainability area. They stood for a while staring at the blackened trees and the razed area where the house had stood. I felt that they were making judgments about whether the grief-stricken, middle-aged woman standing before them should even be allowed to rebuild in such an isolated, devastated location.

I waited as they wandered around to peer down towards the creek, then to scan the opposite hillside and its burden of blackened forest. I watched their eyes flicker across the bunker area and then swing around to take in the tumbled chimney and the steps-to-nowhere.

REBUILD

I stood quietly on the brick porch and I waited. This was Waldene and it was all that I had left of Barry and I would rebuild and I would not be judged by them.

The men eventually regrouped beside me. They were concerned about the steep driveway. They could not locate the original septic tank but decided that it would not meet current regulations in any case. They asked me to describe what size cottage I had in mind. They asked about the original source of power to the block. They marvelled that the cottage had used gas lighting. They listened as I described the recently installed solar panels that had powered the stereo and my laptop. They discussed the difficulty of trying to build on a site without electricity connected.

I gained the impression that while each was an expert in their own field, they were somewhat challenged to collectively map out the steps I would need to go through in order to have a completely fitted out, plumbed and powered cottage rebuilt on the site. They discussed issues back and forth with little resolution. The modern septic system apparently required more level land for drainage purposes than I had available on the sloping block. They doubted the septic issue could be solved. I watched and listened, hating their pessimistic attitudes.

Of course it could be done, I thought. Barry and I had trekked all over the world. We had been in any variety of toilets on remote bush tracks. I wondered what they thought I had been using for a toilet system for the past seven months at Waldene while I waited for permission to begin rebuilding.

I interrupted them to ask where I should start the process of rebuilding. I knew nothing about how gas tanks or solar panels worked, nor did I have much knowledge of generators, septic tanks or water pumps. Barry had always managed all those things.

I said that I felt somewhat overwhelmed with the whole task of rebuilding without him, but that was the hand I had been dealt and I just needed their guidance. I would make the phone calls, organise the meetings and handle the paperwork. I just needed to know what steps I had to take.

The team looked somewhat surprised. Perhaps they had incorrectly assumed that their conversation had served to show me the impossibility of rebuilding.

The building inspector took the lead. He suggested that the first thing that I should do was to contact SP AusNet, the electrical supplier to the area, to determine the possibility and cost of having electricity brought to the block. Connecting to the electricity supply would significantly simplify the whole task of rebuilding.

Having provided this specific suggestion, the team and I parted company. As they walked back up the driveway I wondered what they were saying about me and my decision to rebuild in spite of their emphasis on the difficulties involved. They did not understand. There was no choice in this for me. This was something that I must do, regardless of how long it might take or how complicated it might become. I would rebuild even if I had to hammer in every nail myself.

I wrote to SP AusNet asking if there was a possibility of getting electricity to Waldene and requesting an estimate of cost. Once I knew that, I would be better able to work out how to go about rebuilding.

Monday 17 August 2009
SP AusNet responded to my request regarding the cost of connecting electricity to Waldene. They thanked me for my inquiry and provided a 'Preliminary Estimate' based on a document that I had completed and sent to them. The letter further advised that

to obtain a 'Firm Offer' I would need to pay a non-refundable project fee of $550 (GST inclusive). The non-refundable fee would be deducted from the total cost if I proceeded with the work.

The enormously high estimate appeared to shout scornfully at me from the page:

> We estimate your contribution to these works to be within the range of $69 200 to $83 900 GST inclusive.

I was shocked at the cost. This was far beyond what I had anticipated. It became evident why Barry had opted for alternate sources of energy when he had first built Waldene decades ago. I would likewise have to do without electricity in the rebuilt cottage. This would make the task of building that much harder, but even at $69 000, the cost of installing electricity was prohibitive.

The neighbouring blocks on Humevale Road only contained rough, jerry-built shacks. The property owners were unlikely to be willing to share the cost of connecting power to the area.

Saturday 29 August 2009

A small team of people from the SES worked all day at Waldene cutting up many of the fallen trees scattered around the house site. I was worried about the multitude of large wood piles that they were creating. While grateful that the fallen trees were being cut up, I doubted that I would have the strength to drag all the logs into a safe location or eventually be brave enough to set fire to them.

As the men worked, I stacked the smaller branches back into the place where the wood pile used to be. The neatly stacked wood pile appeared to be waiting for a house, a wood stove or a fireplace. I already had a brick porch and a set of steps that led to nowhere and now I had a wood pile with no fireplace. Everything seemed to be missing something.

Now and again, somewhere along the valley could be heard the sudden moan of a dead tree relinquishing its grip on the earth and crashing down, unaided by a chainsaw. At other times a small gust of wind felled fragile branches that had not realised they were no longer part of the living. The forest was shedding its skin slowly, suddenly and dangerously.

19

Tuesday 1 September 2009
My diary entry for Tuesday says:

> BJ has been gone almost 7 months. I'm still staggering on – why or to where, I don't know.

Wednesday 2 September 2009
My caseworker, David, visited and we talked through everything that had happened and everything I was feeling about the Royal Commission. David confessed months ago that he knew little about building and building regulations but he could pass on information to me and help me research whatever I needed to find out. Today, however, I was grateful for his outstanding ability to listen. Living alone as I now do, he has proven to be a wonderful sounding board for my thoughts and he helps me to gain a clearer perspective on things.

After David left, I received a phone call from Gus Carfi, the counsellor from the Royal Commission. He was ringing to check how I was feeling and if I needed any further assistance. We spoke for a while and Gus said that he would ring me back in a couple of weeks. He made me promise to phone him if I needed to talk. 'Anytime,' he said, 'Day or night. It doesn't matter.' I thanked him for his offer.

Friday 4 September 2009
Lana Kolyunski, the Commission's community engagement manager, phoned me. She wanted to warn me that next Wednesday

(9 September) the news reports on television might run items about the three people who perished in bunkers during the Black Saturday fires. She thought that I might be upset if I watched the reports, particularly if I was not forewarned that they were to be shown.

I thanked Lana for her thoughtfulness and explained that I rarely watched the news nowadays. I was working in Coober Pedy next week and was due to fly home late Wednesday. I noted my diary not to watch the news, just in case.

Wednesday 9 September 2009

A letter from the Royal Commission was waiting for me when I arrived back from Coober Pedy. The letter thanked me for providing consent for the State Coroner of Victoria to release my contact details to the Commission. This was yet another confusing bureaucratic tangle, given my recent testimony at the Commission. Obviously two different streams of clerical officers were working on two different components of the one case.

The Commission wanted to inform me that it would soon commence its examination into the causes and circumstances of the Black Saturday deaths. The hearings were to be 'largely reliant on statements and evidence gathered by the police'.

The letter went on to advise that the hearings would commence in September for the Beechworth, Bendigo and Churchill fires followed by hearings into the Murrindindi and Kilmore fires. It was anticipated that the hearings would continue until approximately mid May 2010. The letter assured me that Lana Kolyunski from the Commission would contact me over the next few weeks to discuss the process in more detail.

I was puzzled as to what else the Commission could possibly

want from me. I had made endless formal statements, proffered relevant photographs, spoken with police and solicitors and even presented testimony at the interim Commission hearing. I had nothing else to say or to show them that could advance their understanding of what happened at Waldene that day.

Wednesday 16 September 2009

Detective Grant phoned to discuss my original statement to police. He said that I had told police that I phoned Barry after work from Greensborough at about 5.30 pm. The phone records showed that Barry had only received a call from the Greensborough phone at 4.28 pm that lasted for almost five minutes.

Detective Grant wanted to know if my original estimate of 5.30 pm could be mistaken. I admitted that I was making a very rough estimate at the time. I had finished work in Parkville about 3.30 pm and then been driven to Greensborough by a colleague. With hindsight, the 4.28 pm time was no doubt correct. Detective Grant said that he would have to revise my statement; he would contact me in the next few weeks to make an appointment to have the revised statement signed and witnessed.

Thursday 17 September 2009

Gus Carfi, the counsellor from the Royal Commission, phoned me again. We chatted and I told him that I was coping all right. He reminded me to contact him if I felt I would like someone to talk to in the future.

Later in an email to a friend I made the following postscript:

> PS *The psychologist from the Bushfire Commission phoned today to see how I was going. I daren't say. They put people in institutions for feeling like I do at the moment ... sigh*

20

Wednesday 30 September 2009

I realised that if I was to be of any use at Waldene I would need to gain experience in towing the trailer. I needed to be able to collect timber and gardening supplies. I wanted to find out what was involved in going to the tip. If I was unable to burn all the fallen trees and branches at Waldene, perhaps I could take them to the tip.

Early this morning after hitching the trailer onto 'Barry's car' I loaded it with some hard rubbish from the house at Greensborough including all the discarded wood from the original small bathroom cabinet. I tied a tarpaulin over the load using metres of rope that I had bought especially for the task. Unable to remember any of the knots that I had learned as a Girl Guide I was reduced to securing the load with numerous, cumbersome shoelace knots. It was not a pretty sight but it was secure. I wondered how long it would take me to undo all the knots when I arrived at the tip.

My heart was thumping as I drove out onto the road with my loaded trailer. Keeping to the left-hand lane and stealing glances in the rear and side mirrors, I set out on the 14-kilometre drive to the tip. Within a few kilometres I had to pull over. The tarpaulin had come free in one corner and was flapping wildly. Somewhat embarrassedly, while cars flashed past me, I struggled to secure the escaped tarpaulin beneath some of the bulbous knots I had tied.

Back in the car, I eased out onto the road again. A bit further along a passing car honked and the driver gestured that he had something to tell me. I pulled over again. He pulled in behind me and explained that one of the wheels on the trailer was wobbling. I stared down at the wheels. They looked fine. The driver suggested that perhaps the rim was buckled. Not sure what a rim was, I agreed with him and said that I would get it seen to. I thanked him for letting me know. The driver returned to his car and smiling and waving to me, he drove away.

I began to panic. Me towing a trailer to the tip; what had I been thinking? This was lunacy. I knew nothing about mechanics. What was a rim? The tyre looked fine. I walked around from one side of the trailer to the other, trying to compare the two tyres to determine what a rim was by detecting some difference between the two.

I wondered what would happen if I continued on to the tip. What was the potential outcome of driving with a buckled rim? Would I get a flat tyre? I had never changed a flat tyre. Although I had completed a basic car maintenance lesson years ago, I had been terrified when told that locating the car-jack in the wrong place could damage the car badly. I gleaned that jacking up a vehicle with a misplaced jack is akin to pressing on the wrong part of the chest when resuscitating a person and breaking their ribs as a result.

I stood at the side of the road for some time trying to decide what to do. I sat in the car and wondered who I might phone to ask for advice. It was a weekday and everyone would be at work. The street directory showed me that I was about halfway to the tip. That meant 7 kilometres to drive back to Greensborough or 21 kilometres if I did the round trip to the tip anyway. It was too risky. Sadly I turned the car around and drove back to Greensborough.

That evening Heath came to look at the trailer. He explained what the tyre rim was and assured me that although the rim might be slightly buckled, I could still tow the trailer. He knew that I was desperate to gain experience with the trailer and that my trips would be short and few in the week that it would take him to obtain another rim.

Saturday 3 October 2009

Early in the morning I set off for the tip again, towing the laden trailer with its buckled rim. I was flagged down twice by passing motorists on the way, both anxious to tell me that one wheel on the trailer was wobbling. In both cases I feigned surprise, thanked them and said that I would get it fixed when I returned home. My nerves were stretched to the limit when I turned off the road and through the large gates at the tip.

I drove carefully onto the weighbridge, as proud as if I was driving a road-train. I was Miss Mouse and yet here I was doing stuff that grown men sometimes have trouble doing. I was pleased with myself. Barry would be so proud of me.

I paid my fee and then followed the directions to arrive at the dumping area. The attendant gestured for me to drive a sweeping circle and then reverse back to where he was standing. I was to reverse in between two other cars with trailers that were in the process of being emptied by their owners.

The sweeping circle was easy, but reversing the trailer was a new experience. It seemed impossible. I had no control over the trailer as I reversed and corrected multiple times. The attendant watched, amused by my antics. Finally he came over and I sheepishly wound down my window to explain that I had never reversed a trailer before.

He grinned. 'That's okay, love ... least you're willing to say so. Most blokes won't admit it an' it takes 'em ages to back in.'

I went to open my door. 'Can you back it in for me?' I asked.

'Nah. Not allowed to get into anyone's car,' he said. 'Might get accused of theft or something,' he explained with a hint of contempt. 'I'll just help ya through the window.'

With that, his dark, scarred hand took hold of my steering wheel. 'Okay, love, just reverse her slowly.' He walked beside the car, turning the steering wheel slightly as we went. I was amazed at his skill. Walking forward he steered my car and trailer through the driver's side window as we reversed. I laughed at the absurdity of it all.

'There ya go,' he said, letting go of the steering wheel to wander over to a newly arrived truck.

I untied all of my knots, pulled off the tarpaulin and following the lead of the men on either side of me, dragged my rubbish out and threw it into the compacting area.

I was dragging rubbish around at the tip. I was doing something I had never done before. I was working with the men rather than giggling with the girls. I was towing a trailer and I felt strong and happy and empowered. This day, this achievement, may have seemed rough and dirty to an onlooker but inside, for me, it was pivotal. It was my 'first blood', an initiation of sorts. I had crossed over from something that I had been to something that was so much more. I would rebuild Waldene even if I had to do it myself. Today I believed this pledge more so than any time since losing Barry.

21

Tuesday 6 October 2009

My darling would have turned 60 years old today. I knew that had he lived Barry would never have let me organise a 60th birthday party for him. He would not have approved of being 60.

Dekky, Stewie, Barry's ashes and I spent the day sitting on the brick porch at Waldene. I had found a diary that Barry had written in 2002 in my office drawer. He had written it when we holidayed in Greece. I read the diary aloud to the bears and the ashes and the forest. It was a delight to see Barry's beautiful handwriting on the page. I traced some of the firm lettering with my fingertips. Each page conjured up a host of memories. Once again I plodded behind him along the streets of Athens, weighed down by my backpack. I leant against him on the train to Piraeus, made love to him in the morning sunshine in a room in Paros and stood beside him to watch the sunset over the ocean at Santorini.

In the evening Judy came for a 60th birthday celebration. We stood next to a bookcase, which is where Barry always finished up at parties, and toasted him with champagne. Then we had dinner at his favourite restaurant. We ordered the smoked eggplant dip that he loved so much, even though neither Jude nor I really like it.

When we returned to Greensborough, Jude produced two little cupcakes each bearing a candle. I offered to light them then and there but Judy said she wanted me to have them. She left and I sat staring at the cupcakes. I realise that she probably intended them to represent one for me and one for Barry. I lit the candles and sang 'Happy Birthday'. The house looked on, cold, dark and impersonal. I went to bed crying.

Wednesday 7 October 2009

All my phone conversations with the Whittlesea Council and all my visits to builders display cottages since Grocon had cleared Waldene had ended in a confusion of ambiguous suggestions, uncertainty regarding changes to the building regulations as a result of the fires, and frustrations about the lack of power to the site and the difficulty of getting large machinery down the steep and rapidly deteriorating driveway.

On 31 August when I had talked to Gus Carfi, the counsellor attached to the Victoria Bushfires Royal Commission, I had told him that I might build a bus shelter at the site in which I could sit and wait while the bureaucrats worked out the new 'game rules'.

I had told Gus back then that a shed, though easier to build, would be too 'closed in'. However, now after six months of dragging the trailer from Greensborough to Waldene every time I wanted to bring a wheelbarrow, mower, gardening tools or even water to the block, the suggestion to build a shed was gaining traction in my mind.

At least if I had a shed I could store tools, I thought. I could buy a tank and collect water from the roof of a shed. I could even put some simple furniture in a shed and stay overnight if I wanted. A friend had bought me a small stove that worked off tiny gas canisters when I began talking about the possibility of a shed. I bought some solar lights.

In my mind I could see great joy in being able to sleep at Waldene again. The facilities would be very basic and would not be sufficient for much more than an overnight stay, but how wonderful that would be. It would be like when Barry and I had been camping, but with even more protection afforded by Colorbond walls and a roof.

I began searching the internet for shed sizes and prices. I did not want to spend so much that it prevented me from ever building a cottage, but I wanted to get the largest shed that I could obtain for a modest price. I would locate it on the ledge exactly where the original shed had been. I would be able to look at it and know that I had started to rebuild. The thought filled me with happiness.

I emailed a shed company in Coolaroo and they promised to send me a brochure. In the meantime I pored over their internet brochure with as much joy as a princess studies the plans for a palace. While the bureaucrats decided what the rules would be, I would build a shed in which I could wait and dream.

Wednesday 21 October 2009

When David, my caseworker, arrived I had a number of brochures about sheds and some information about water tanks to show him. I had been up at Waldene pacing and measuring out possible shed sizes. Although I was enthusiastic about purchasing a shed, I had absolutely no idea how to have it transported to Waldene or how to get it built. I wondered if a building permit would be needed. Some of the shed brochures said that the landowner was responsible for obtaining any necessary local council permits. I wondered if a shed was something that I could put together myself or would I need a builder.

David was enthusiastic but admitted that his knowledge of such things was probably on a par with mine. He copied down lots of information from the brochures and took notes from our conversation. He said that he would ask around the office and see what he could find out that might be of help.

Later that afternoon, David rang back and told me about a scheme that was operating to help people rebuild after the bushfires. He gave me the contact details for the Whittlesea area. I phoned immediately and made an appointment to see Marcus Worrall at the 'Hub' in Whittlesea at 11 am on Wednesday 28 October. I was feeling very excited. At last I was going to begin to rebuild Waldene. I was already ashamed that it had taken so long, yet at the same time I could not see how I could have speeded up the process.

Thursday 22 October 2009
A cheque representing the settlement of Barry's estate arrived in the mail. This meant that I would no longer have to deal with Daniel or his solicitor. I renewed my personal vow that as soon as I was emotionally strong enough, I would stand face to face with him and make sure that he realised that his treatment of me since the fires would never have been approved by Barry. I wanted him to suffer a crushing guilt for the remainder of his life.

Monday 26 October 2009
Major Glenys Ford from the Salvation Army phoned. She said that the work with the Black Saturday bushfires and the aftermath had taken its toll on her. She had decided to retire.

I apologised for my part in this, but Glenys graciously laughed it off, saying that she had been involved in a lot of other things as part of the bushfire work and that I was in no way responsible for her decision. I thought back to that day in February when she was supposed to be making tea and sandwiches for weary firefighters but instead was given me to deal with. I felt sure the day had not been easy for her.

Glenys invited me to her retirement function in November. I explained that I was not very good emotionally at large functions and that my crying would upset people. She insisted that no-one would mind. I felt somewhat obligated to this lady who had looked after me on the very worst day of my life. Although a total stranger, she had not faltered in her care and kindness towards me.

22

Wednesday 28 October 2009

The Hub at Whittlesea turned out to be a large portable building that had been transported to a vacant block in the township. There was a crowd of people in the reception area and I had to wait my turn to speak to the receptionist. The Hub appeared to be housing a range of support services and organisations relevant to people affected by the fire. There was an endless supply of boiling water, cups, tea, coffee and biscuits. In a makeshift waiting area, people sat quietly talking and flicking through the stacks of brochures and pamphlets that were piled on the centre table. People emerged from around partitioning to call names and people came and went. It seemed to me that this was a place where things got done.

A man stepped into the foyer and called my name. In an accent that hinted of a New Zealand origin, he introduced himself as Marcus Worrall. I followed him into a large room with a row of desks stretching around its perimeter. Each desk afforded one chair for its resident worker and one or two on its opposite side for the clients. There was little room between each table and as a result, little privacy. Seemingly oblivious of this, the workers and clients leant towards each other across the tables, their heads bent in earnest conversations.

Marcus steered me towards a table that held a laptop and some papers. He squeezed in behind the table and gestured for me to take the single seat opposite him. I sat down and he gave me a boyish grin. 'Sorry it's a bit crowded in here,' he said, stating the obvious.

Marcus said that his role was to offer building advice to people wanting to rebuild after the bushfires. He told me that he was one of a team of rebuilding advisors who had been appointed by the Department of Planning and Community. The rebuilding advisors were stationed at various locations including Kilmore, Marysville and Kinglake. Marcus and a few other rebuilding advisors were responsible for looking after the Kinglake-Whittlesea area. I stared at the logo on his shirt. It bore the promissory state government logo: 'We Will Rebuild'.

Marcus opened a large writing pad and asked me for my name and contact details. The page was blank and I knew instantly what was about to happen. Marcus smiled up at me, unaware of the flood of tears that he was about to unleash.

'So,' he said with pen poised, 'What damage did your house suffer in the fires?'

I looked down at my fingers clutching my backpack on my knees. I tried to think where I should start. Should I tell Marcus about the steep driveway, or that I needed a special septic tank? Perhaps I should tell him about the cost of putting electricity onto the block. I wondered if I should say that I had decided I would be happy with a shed.

The tears started to sting at the corners of my eyes. I wanted to begin optimistically so that he would not try to convince me not to rebuild. I already had the Council and some friends and relations hinting at the futility of me even considering rebuilding. How could they begin to understand that I must?

Marcus sat waiting for me to speak. 'Did you lose your house in the fires?' he probed gently.

I looked across at him. 'I lost my partner in the fire. The house … everything. I have to rebuild. But I don't know how.' Then I broke down completely. I felt like I had been trying for such a long time and yet here I was, still at the beginning. I was sitting opposite another stranger asking for help to get back something of 'yesterday'. My world was so tiny, so constantly repeating; like a blunt mower going backwards and forwards endlessly over the same small patch of grass without ever cutting a single blade.

Marcus was apologetic. He tried to calm me, with little success. He turned his laptop around to face me and brought up his screensaver. The chubby outline of a giggling baby danced onto the screen. 'Look at him,' said Marcus proudly. 'That's my son and he was born just after the bushfires. That's gotta give you hope doesn't it?'

I recognised the pride in his voice. He was trying to give me a small piece of the miracle contained in his first child. Here was the centre of his own joy and he was trying to share it with me. I could not surface from the sea of tears that now engulfed me.

Marcus leapt to his feet and told me to keep looking at the baby and he would be back in a minute. He squeezed back between the tables and disappeared in the direction of the reception area. I sat hunched over my bag crying, oblivious of what was going on around me in that crowded room.

Marcus returned with a middle-aged woman. He introduced her and said she was a social worker and it would be good if I went to speak with her in a private room before speaking with him. He grinned at me. 'She'll make you a cuppa tea and give you a bickie, Sue. I'll come and have a talk with you a bit later and we'll see what we can do.'

I stood up and, apologising to Marcus, followed the social worker out to a small private room beyond the reception area. I can no longer remember what the social worker and I talked about. I imagine that I told her everything that had happened to me since

I hung up the phone after talking with Barry on Black Saturday. Given the state I was in, the facts probably tumbled out in a tangled mess that made little sense. After some time had elapsed and I had stopped crying, the social worker left me for a moment to go and speak to Marcus. I sat waiting, wondering if they would return and say there was nothing that could be done for me.

Marcus and the social worker did return to speak with me and Marcus went on to support me in a long and difficult journey for the next few years. That day, Marcus gave me a list of people who were authorised to conduct Bushfire Attack Level (BAL) ratings on properties. He told me that before anything could be done by way of rebuilding, it would be necessary to obtain a BAL rating for the property at Waldene. The BAL rating was a new initiative as a result of the Victoria Bushfire Royal Commission.

Marcus said that he would leave me to select and contact an assessor and organise to have the property rated. I was to phone him when I had made all the arrangements. Here was a beginning at last.

I was pleased to be given a specific task to do that formed part of the rebuilding at Waldene. I appreciated that Marcus had made his explanation simple and given me some responsibility, but at the same time, asked me to check in so he could map my progress.

At a later date Marcus told me that he had previously been 'just a builder', but his deliberate efforts to give me some control, some power in this horrible situation, was worthy of a note in any psychologist's handbook.

In December 2011, before I had managed to rebuild at Waldene, the Department of Planning and Community dissolved most of the rebuilding advisors' positions in the errant belief that they were no longer required. The government had incorrectly assumed that anyone who wanted to rebuild would have done so in the three years since Black Saturday. Marcus was among those who were retrenched. I wrote him a letter of thanks to express my immense gratitude for all that he did for me.

Sunday 1 November 2009

My diary entry shows a sketch of a crying face. The text alongside the sketch says:

> *I survived until now – ONLY JUST.*
> *7.2.09 – 30.10.09*
> *8½ months*
> *Am I nearly there???*

Thursday 5 November 2009

Anthony Wright, a BAL assessor, met me at Waldene this morning. I worked to restore some of the garden beds while Mr Wright wandered around the property taking measurements with special tools and making a sketch of the building 'apron', the slope of the land and the density of the surrounding vegetation.

The five BAL categories range from BAL12.5 at the lower end of fire risk to BAL-FZ (flame zone) at the highest level of risk. The checklist that the BAL assessors investigate involves making determinations about the type of vegetation and the slope of the land. Flat land covered in tussocks or moorland attracts a lower risk than steeply sloping land covered in forest. Waldene stretches across the side of a steep hill amidst the forest. I doubted that a blind man would have trouble classifying it as BAL-FZ.

Mr Wright returned again a few days later to take further measurements at Waldene. He talked with me about my plans for rebuilding and stuck some temporary pegs in the ground to mark the corner posts of a small cottage that I had been thinking of rebuilding on the original house site. He suggested that I pay someone to remove a large tree stump that remained after the SES had cut down a tree near the brick porch. Mr Wright also took me up to the roadside to show me where I might realign the driveway to reduce its steepness.

I was unsure what power or influence the BAL rating or Mr Wright had in the whole rebuilding process but I was happy that he seemed to think rebuilding was not out of the realm of possibility. Between Marcus and Mr Wright's attitudes, I was filled with optimism.

Friday 6 November 2009

Since my last discussion with Detective Grant I had been thinking hard about the phone call between Barry and me on Black Saturday. For some reason I had an image of me speaking to Barry on my mobile phone from the car park before I left work for the day. I had convinced myself that Barry had phoned me while I sat in the passenger seat of my colleague's car. I thought I remembered opening the door to cool the car down as we spoke while I waited for my colleague to finish farewelling some other workmates.

I could not remember what Barry and I had spoken about. Perhaps we had talked about what we would have for dinner, perhaps we had spoken about the weather? I could not get the image out of my mind. I wanted to know if I had spoken to him twice on that last day; once in the car park on my mobile and then later at 4.28 pm when I phoned him on the Greensborough landline.

I emailed Detective Grant asking if there was some way that he could check the records for me. An excerpt from my email appears below and shows my state of mind:

> *Sorry to be a nuisance but a vague memory of a phone call from Barry to my mobile while I was in the zoo car park keeps niggling on my mind. Sometimes I think that perhaps I may have even phoned him from the car park. It doesn't matter to anyone but me. But I'd like to know for certain if we spoke on my mobile as well as on the landline; two conversations with Barry on that last day would be better than one.*

Monday 9 November 2009

Finally I had to admit that I probably needed some counselling help. I was making some progress in that I was no longer operating in a mental fog, but I was still crying almost without provocation. While the tears no longer worried me, they were proving awkward and uncomfortable for people working with me. I had held off seeking counselling for fear that any record of receiving mental health treatment might have the potential to cause problems for me in future employment options.

I was painfully aware that my friends were starting to weary of hearing me talk endlessly about Barry. I had tried to stop myself but everything reminded me of him and it was difficult not to mention him whenever an opportunity presented. It was as if talking about him helped to keep him alive or at least a reality.

The Department of Human Services had posted me six counselling vouchers back in August. At that time I had decided that I did not need them and I had filed them away. Now, however, I visited my local doctor hoping that she would offer me some sort of quick fix.

The doctor suggested that I might need drugs and/or counselling. I flatly refused the drugs. I did not want to be foggy and dazed. I had to be alert to make sure that I stayed focused on rebuilding at Waldene. She referred me to a nearby counsellor, Kylie Wainwright.

I returned to Greensborough a little disappointed in myself. How could I have fallen this low? I had always had a strong constitution, even though I was very sensitive and prone to tears in emotional situations. Barry would not approve of psychologists. During my younger years, I had completed four years of psychology studies across two different university courses. Had I completed all four years at one institution I could have been a psychologist myself. 'Physician, heal thyself' I could hear Barry saying. I was a disappointment to myself tonight.

Saturday 14 November 2009
Today was my 56th birthday and I woke up feeling sad. It was my first birthday without Barry. I had a 'Birthday Girl' badge and card that he had once given me. I pinned the badge onto my T-shirt and wore it all day and put the card beside my computer so that I could pretend he had just given it to me.

A straggle of friends began popping in at Greensborough after lunch. I was indebted to them for thinking to visit me on this special day. Three friends remained to sleep over for the night. We had takeaway for dinner and they presented me with a cake and candles. After singing 'Happy Birthday', I cut the cake and made a wish.

One friend asked me what I had wished for. I burst into tears. 'I wished I was dead,' I sobbed. Later that night I told my friends that 'I feel like I am walking along the edge of a cliff all the time and I don't know what will happen – will I fall or walk on?'

Wednesday 17 November 2009

Detective Grant phoned to make an appointment to visit me. He has revised my original statement so that it now shows that I estimated that I had spoken to Barry about 4.30 pm on Black Saturday. This was a better match with the phone records.

In response to my email about the phone calls, Detective Grant had checked the records and found that besides my 4.30 pm call, Barry had taken only two other calls on Black Saturday. One had been from Daniel at 2 pm for less than a minute. The other caller was from an unknown person. Barry had not answered that incoming call. Detective Grant asked if I recognised the other phone number. I did not. (Later, the police traced the call back to a market research company.)

No phone calls had been made from Waldene that day. That meant that I could not have spoken to Barry on the phone in the car park after work. It was another piece of the puzzle cleared up, but I was saddened to think that the image I had of speaking to Barry at another time on Black Saturday had turned out to be a figment of my fuddled imagination; a tiny death in its own right.

Detective Grant asked if I could collect some items for him including some of the photos that I had provided to the Royal Commission. We made an appointment for him to return on 24 November.

Later that day I had my first appointment with psychologist Kylie Wainwright. I felt embarrassed and ashamed as I waited at the counter to have my details recorded by the receptionist. I was now in the 'Suffering Depression' category. I would have to begin at the beginning and tell everything all over again. Ms Wainwright would probably poke and probe my psyche and try to make me 'wake up to myself'. I sat at the door of the waiting room that led out to the car park. I stared at my car in the parking lot and toyed with the idea of quietly slipping away before my name was called.

Kylie, I pondered. How can you talk seriously to someone called Kylie? It was a teenage child's name, like Kylie Minogue. I began to panic. This was a terrible mistake. I did not need to talk through stuff with a 'Kylie'.

My name was called. It was Ms Wainwright. It was too late to escape. I followed her down the corridor and into a small room with two armchairs and some children's toys piled in the corner. She asked me to call her Kylie, enquired if I wanted a glass of water and said that she hoped I would not mind if she had one. I liked her instantly. She seemed ordinary, unpretentious and was more mature than her name suggested.

I clutched my backpack on my lap and waited for her to begin. I spent an hour with Kylie and she did not take any notes during the session. She asked me to tell her about Black Saturday. She wanted to know all about Barry. She laughed at some his funny antics and was impressed by his intelligence. I was pleased that I had described him the way that he had seemed to me. I felt very proud of him. I told her that I still puzzled over what Barry had ever seen in me.

The hour flew by. I could have stayed talking to Kylie. She was a good listener. She did not grow weary of hearing about Barry and about our life together. When I cried she did not fuss; she just waited quietly until I found my way again.

Kylie asked me if I would come and see her again in a week. I agreed, even though I realised that the short time between visits probably meant I was probably more 'depressed' than 'sad'. We made another appointment for the following Wednesday. Kylie told the receptionist to bulk bill me. I was never sure if this was because

I was a bushfire victim, or because I qualified for funding as part of the Beyond Blue mental health initiative, or because Kylie was yet another very kind stranger doing what she could to help me.

Sunday 22 November 2009
The Salvation Army Citadel in Glen Waverley was filled to capacity for Glenys's retirement service. Although we had spoken on the phone numerous times I had only seen Glenys on that day in February when police had handed me into her care.

In the Citadel I recognised Glenys amidst a sea of well-wishers. Seeing me, Glenys pushed through the crowd and caught me in an enormous hug. She insisted that I sit near the front with her family and close friends. She seated me between '... two very kind ladies who know all about you.'

I joined in as the crowd sang hymns and ignoring my tears, the ladies on either side patted my back comfortingly.

Speeches were made and I was humbled when Glenys mentioned my presence in the hall. I was glad I had come, both for Glenys and for myself. As I drove home, I felt joyous and full of hope. Although I am not religious the evening had been wonderfully uplifting.

Tuesday 24 November 2009
Detective Grant called in to have me sign the revised statement regarding the time I had phoned Barry on Black Saturday and to collect the items that he had asked me to assemble for him when last we met.

After he drove away, I thought about the fact that I had been meeting with, being interviewed by, and signing forms about Black Saturday for over nine months now. It seemed amazing that Barry had perished somewhere between 4.35 pm on Saturday 7 February and early the next morning, somewhere within an eighteen-hour time frame, and yet after nine months we were still trying to figure it all out.

At my appointment with Kylie this afternoon I talked about how lengthy the whole process seemed to be. She listened and we discussed why this might be the case. I also talked about the sense of urgency I had about telling Daniel how much grief he had caused me. Kylie asked me if that was a wise thing to do.

It was difficult to explain. I felt that I had been fighting Daniel ever since losing Barry. It seemed almost as if he was jealous of my relationship with Barry. As a result he had all but excluded me from any decision-making regarding Barry's memorial service, his ashes or his will. I had had to struggle to be heard. His attitude had made everything much harder for me than it needed to be. Kylie suggested that if I was to visit Daniel, I should not go alone.

During this session with Kylie she asked me why I always nursed my backpack on my lap instead of putting it on the floor. I began to cry. I opened the backpack and showed her a plastic pocket, thick with documents about Barry. I carried the documents everywhere with me.

They included the power of attorney that had given me passage through the Whittlesea roadblock months earlier, a copy of the police statement I had made with Detective Cartagena and a copy of the recent revised statement signed with Detective Grant. There were some photos of Barry and of Barry and me together, of Waldene before the fire, and of my writing studio. Among the collection was one of the lovely cards that I had organised to be printed for Barry's memorial service.

Kylie asked why I carried the documents with me. I hesitated, smoothing down the curled edges of the plastic pocket as I thought this through. I could not remember making a conscious decision to carry the documents. I could not even explain the selection of certain documents over others.

'I need to have them in case something happens to me,' I blurted out unsure what I meant.

'Why?' Kylie asked.

'In case I die,' I answered from somewhere deep inside me. 'I need people to know who I was.'

Kylie did not push me any further. Even now I am unsure completely what I meant. I still carry the plastic pocket with me and over time have added other items. I cannot explain why some things are included and others are not. I still cannot rationally explain why I need to carry the documents. My most competent explanation even today remains, 'When I die, I need them to know who I was.' And looking back now I think what I meant was that I want them to know that 'I was Barry's Sue'.

23

Friday 27 November 2009

A meeting with Marcus exposed another piece of legislation that had come out of the Royal Commission interim report. Any building at Waldene now also had to have the approval of the CFA in addition to the local council. At the very least, this meant that in the event of a bushfire the property had to enable the CFA trucks to gain access in order to defend any structure on the property.

The BAL assessment showed the driveway had a 15-degree slope and Marcus was concerned that this would probably be too steep for a CFA truck to drive down. I complained to Marcus that the CFA did not come to Waldene on Black Saturday and I would not expect them to come if it happened again. It was too dangerous for volunteers to wind all the way down Humevale Road, given the handful of homes built along it.

Marcus said that the new rules took no account of that. He said that he had spoken to the CFA and had been told to complete a request for special dispensation, given that we were trying to rebuild an established house rather than building anew. Marcus said that he would go out to look at the land and speak again with the CFA to determine what should go into the document. I wondered if the CFA would be kind and reasonable.

Apparently it was also necessary to have a 'site test' done on the soil at Waldene. Marcus gave me the contact details of some companies that conducted the necessary tests and asked me to organise this. I had been told that the reason Grocon had taken the top layer of soil from Waldene was to rid it of potential contaminants resulting from the fire. I had no idea what a site test involved, but I was already learning to jump through whatever bureaucratic hoops I had to if I wanted to rebuild at Waldene.

Tuesday 1 December 2009

A site test had now been conducted. The outcome was a fifteen-page document which, 'roughly summarised', says that the soil is ostensibly 'brown-to-yellow clay'. This was another fact that a blind man could have reported. The document came with an invoice for $418 and a request for payment within seven days. I sent a cheque and phoned Marcus with the 'good news'. I wondered how many of these irritating hurdles stood between me and a cottage.

Friday 4 December 2009

My diary shows that Detective Grant visited me at Greensborough for an hour and a half this morning, but I have no notes that explain the purpose of his visit. Perhaps he was returning some of the items I had provided him with.

When I tried to start my car later in the day, to attend an appointment with Kylie, the battery was flat. I phoned Kylie's receptionist to explain what had happened and to cancel the appointment. A few minutes later rang Kylie me. She offered suggestions for getting the car to start. I was amazed at her 'hands-on' approach. I asked her if she thought I had 'chickened out of my appointment and invented the car trouble as an excuse'. She laughed and said that the thought had not even crossed her mind, but then asked me if that indeed was the situation.

I confirmed that the car was refusing to start and that I was sorry to have to cancel our meeting. We made another appointment for

16 December. Kylie asked me to phone her before then if I felt I needed to talk to her.

Wednesday 9 December 2009
Marcus phoned to say he had lodged the special dispensation request with the CFA. He was hoping to meet a representative from the CFA at Waldene sometime in the next week, if they could organise a time. Marcus said that there was no need for me to be at that meeting, especially given that it would be organised on the run. There was nothing more that we could do about rebuilding until then.

Wednesday 16 December 2009
At my counselling appointment Kylie asked why I was still wearing the red plastic wristband that the police had given me in February to identify bona fide locals at the roadblocks around Whittlesea. I looked sadly at the wristband.

It had originally been a bright slash of red across my wrist. Over the months it had faded from constant exposure to dishwashing and daily showers. It had become brittle and started to snap. Each time it broke I painstakingly taped it back together with cellotape so that I could continue wearing it.

I touched the band lovingly. My eyes filled with tears. 'Barry used to buy me jewels,' I began. 'He started out buying me expensive jewels, but I was too scared to wear them in case I lost them. I told him that he should buy me cheap, plastic jewels that I could wear without being scared. He said that I was the funniest girl he had ever met. He used to buy me a mix of cheap and expensive jewels after that. He laughed when I was so happy with sparkly cheap baubles. He said I was like a bower bird.'

Struggling for the right words I told Kylie that the plastic disintegrating wristband was the last piece of jewellery that Barry would ever 'give' me. I needed it to last as long as it could.

'I know it looks ugly and funny. But I don't care what other people think. I'm not asking them to wear it; just me – and to me it's very special,' I finished and Kylie nodded in agreement.

That evening I went to Mernda Primary School to see the inaugural 'Barry Johnston Award' presented to a graduating Year 6 student. The School Council had created the award for a student who worked diligently all year and was helpful to other students and the teachers. The award was not based on academic achievement but rather for a student who continually endeavoured to do their best at all times.

I had declined an offer to speak at the ceremony knowing that I would be too emotional. Instead, Scott, one of the teachers would speak, as well as the local Member of Parliament, Danielle Green.

I stood with the teachers to hear Scott speak. He spoke with passion and began to falter as he spoke. He ended his speech abruptly and handed the microphone to Ms Green. I was pleased that Ms Green had met Barry before and was aware of his history. She praised his many contributions to the school, and the local area as well as his political efforts as a draft resistor during the Vietnam War era in the 1970s.

As soon as the award had been presented, I thanked the teachers and hurried back to my car. I was too overcome with emotion to remain any longer. That night Scott emailed me a heartfelt apology:

> *Dear Sue, sorry about the speech tonight. I thought it was something I had to do but I stuffed it. But I would have regretted not trying.*
> *Scott.*

Two days later Scott sent me another email.

> *Hey Sue, I just felt sick when I got home from the concert thinking that I'd let Bazz down. I'd geared myself up for months to do the speech thinking that I would regret letting someone else do it. Pushing myself outside that comfort zone was a way of showing Bazz how important he was and I hoped it'd give me some sort of closure at work where everything reminds me of BJ.*
>
> *Yesterday a boy in my class was cleaning desks for me. One of the rags he was using was the old bank bag from Barry's grade 2/3. He read the name on the bag and came to me and said, 'Well done with your speech, I could tell he must have been your mate.'*
>
> *A parent ... told me he felt the presentation was perfect. When I replied that showing emotion like that wasn't very 'Mernda' he said 'anyone with half a brain got the point'.*
>
> *... the girl who was selected (for the award) understood the importance of the award and is very shocked and honoured to be chosen after only a year in Australia. She has a beautiful and strong character and is the sort Barry would have loved teaching.*

I sent the following reply:

> *Scott, it was a lovely speech. I think you're being too hard on yourself. While you may not have said every word you'd written, all the sentiments were there as well as your obvious emotional distress at losing Barry. He certainly would NOT think that you 'let him down'. On the contrary, you did him proud.*
>
> *It's interesting that you felt that making the speech and being outside your comfort zone was a way of showing Barry how important he was to you. I felt exactly the same when it came time to decide if I would speak at his memorial service... Like you, I wanted personally to say the very special things and I knew that I couldn't let someone else read my words. It would be too hideous!*

I took a pill and then stumbled through my speech because it mattered to me to show Barry that for him, I could rise above my own fear.

Perhaps it's a legacy that Barry leaves us all able to be a bit more courageous than we thought we could ever be.

Friday 18 December 2009

It had been a very sad year and now Christmas was here. I felt that I had failed Barry miserably even though I had never stopped trying to progress things. I had told Kylie, my psychologist, that I felt like I was driving at night. I knew that if I looked straight ahead I would be blinded by all the oncoming lights and unable to move forward. Instead I had to keep my gaze lowered, looking at the small things around me with just a hint of what lay ahead gleaned from the glow at the edge of the lights.

I could do the small things only as long as I did not look up. The enormity of what lay ahead would prove debilitating if I was to consider it in earnest.

'But you can't go back. You know that, don't you?' Kylie asked me.

'Yes. But I don't have to go on either, if I don't want to.'

'What do you mean?' Kylie was puzzled.

'People think you have to brush yourself off and go on; get back in the race. But I could just build a little cottage – beside the road that the race is being run on. I could see the people, but not actually be in the race. I wouldn't be going back, but I wouldn't be going forward either.' I smiled, happy with the image I had described.

'But what would you be doing?' Kylie probed.

I smiled wickedly. 'I'd be waiting … waiting for Barry to come back and get me.'

That afternoon I bought a lightweight, two-person tent for $39.

It was my Christmas present to me. I had decided that I would sleep at Waldene on Christmas night. I was scared, but my need to be at Waldene was stronger than my fear of sleeping there alone in a tent at night.

Saturday 19 December 2009
This morning I sat quietly and wrote a five-minute speech to Daniel. I would not rest until I had fulfilled the promise that I had made to myself about confronting him. This was something that I had to do for my own sanity. The estate had been settled and he no longer held any power over me. Christmas was close and I wanted to rob him of his right to feel sentimental about the loss of Barry at this time. I wanted to tell him how disappointed Barry would have been at his treatment of me throughout this ordeal.

I had decided to drive the hour and a half to Daniel's property. I would knock at the door of his house and when he answered I would say simply and clearly what I needed to say, then I would leave.

I looked down at my speech. It was too long to memorise. Taking another sheet of paper, I listed the key points. I highlighted key words. I felt like a student cramming for a final exam.

As I was getting dressed, I recited the key points in my mind. I was confident that I could say what I needed within a few minutes, which I reasoned, was probably all the time Daniel would grant me.

Judy phoned and I told her what I was doing. She insisted on accompanying me. She said that she would drive us there because she thought that I would probably be pretty emotional on the return trip.

As we drove along the country roads, Judy made me recite my speech and quizzed me about how I might respond to interjections that Daniel might make. I was glad she was with me. My heart was thumping and my breath was coming fast as we turned onto the unmade road that wound around to Daniel's property. I was terrified but determined.

The gateway to the property was closed and padlocked. We hopped out of the car and stared disappointedly down the long driveway. The house was not visible from the road. We dialled Daniel's phone but were transferred to his message bank. We speculated about whether he and Sharna had just gone shopping or if they were away for the Christmas holidays.

Disappointed, we drove back to Greensborough. It had been a long day with no outcome. I was exhausted from the flood of adrenaline that had been coursing through my veins all day. At Judy's insistence, I promised to contact her so that she could drive me when I decided to make a return visit.

Sunday 20 December 2009

My diary entry for this day said:

> I feel VERY sad today!
> I don't think I'm going to make it much longer.
> I miss Barry so much.

Tuesday 22 December 2009

I left Greensborough early and drove to Daniel's alone. I deliberately did not call Judy because I did not want to waste another day of her time if Daniel was not at home. His phone was still diverting to message bank when I had phoned last night.

All the way there, I recited my speech. I had the typed dot points on the seat beside me. In my head I prioritised the dot points just in case I was not going to be given much time to say anything. I was a nervous wreck, but I was equally sure that this was something I had to do before I could move on at Waldene.

I turned onto the unmade road. Daniel's gates were open! I parked the car on the roadside and tried to calm myself. I took another look at my notes before starting the car up again. Slowly I drove through the gates and along the winding driveway into the circular parking bay outside the house. My heart was thumping so loudly that I thought it would come through my T-shirt. My hands were moist on the steering wheel.

Daniel would have been able to see my car approaching for the last few hundred metres. I wondered if he felt a moment of deja vu at seeing what appeared to be 'Barry's car' moving along his driveway. I parked in the parking bay.

As I sat readying myself, a door at the side of the house crashed open. Turning to see what this meant, I caught sight of Daniel, storming authoritatively towards where I was parked.

I opened the car door and hopped out. At the sight of me, he hesitated momentarily. I got the impression that he had thought the car was being driven by some idle traveller, or perhaps his hesitation was shock at seeing me.

Standing beside my car I began, 'I've come to be sure you know that you were no friend of Barry's.'

'Oh, go away!' Daniel said.

'Don't you grieve for him at Christmas or even think about him. You're not worthy to lick his boots,' I continued, glaring hard into his eyes.

'Oh go away or I'll call the police,' he threatened.

'That would be good. Go on then,' I replied, deviating slightly from my planned speech. I was feeling out of control but would not back down this time.

Daniel turned and hurried back towards his house. Over his shoulder he called, 'Go away!'

I yelled at his disappearing frame, 'I hate you and so would Barry … and if the situation was reversed and Barry had to look after Sharna you know he'd have handled it differently!'

Daniel disappeared around the corner of his patio, a banging door signifying the end of our conversation.

So that was it. I had waited a long time for this few minutes. I had said what I needed to say and now Daniel knew, and I knew that he knew. There could be no doubt in his mind. I stood staring up into the sky and breathing for a few moments. I felt immensely relieved and lighthearted.

I drove my car slowly back down the long driveway. I parked outside the gates, and on the back of my dot point page, I scribbled down exactly what I had managed to say to Daniel. I wanted to be able to look back in years to come and be comforted to see that I had made my message very clear.

That night I slept soundly. Daniel no longer existed to me.

Wednesday 23 December 2009

David, my case worker, visited and then later I had an appointment with Kylie. They were both amazed that I had visited Daniel alone and made my speech.

Friday 25 December 2009

When I arrived at Waldene in the early afternoon on Christmas Day, the sun was shining and I felt ridiculously happy. I had brought 'Barry' and the teddies, my pillowcase of memorabilia, a fold-up chair, an esky of treats, some red wine and a battery-operated CD player on which to play some of Barry's favourite opera music. I pitied everyone who was spending Christmas Day with people they did not particularly like. I could not think of one other place on earth that I would rather be. The day was all the better for being alone here, to listen to the breeze, to hear myself think and to revel in the silence.

I walked around the site for a while making more plans for the garden and wondering how to improve some little steps I had started to cut into the slope down to where the shed used to be. I turned on the opera music, poured some wine and sat in the chair to savour the day.

Just before dusk I erected the little tent. To my horror I found that the ground was too hard to take the tent pegs. I carried the tent from place to place trying to find some soft soil. The sky was darkening when I hit on the idea of securing the tent inside the secret garden. The tent floor spanned the brick paving, allowing me to secure the tent pegs in the soft soil around the azalea bulbs. As I worked to secure the tent, the front row of paving stones collapsed. The retaining wall that had secured them had perished in the fire leaving them no support.

Working quickly by torchlight I dragged and rolled some cut tree stumps into place to secure the remaining paving. It was not pretty but it would be hold for the night. With a thin camping mattress and my sleeping bag inside it, the tent was complete. I placed two charged solar lights at the door. It looked a very cheerful and cosy scene.

One more glass of wine on the brick porch and it was time for bed. I glanced around at the dark forbidding landscape. I was scared but I would stay. The worst had already happened to me.

Epilogue

By Christmas 2010 I had succeeded in having a large shed built at Waldene – somewhere to store my tools, a stretcher and a small stove so that I could begin staying overnight. At last I could work on the garden in earnest.

The findings from the Royal Commission were eventually translated into government legislation and local councils expanded their rules to incorporate new planning and building requirements.

In April 2012 the necessary BAL-FZ building materials had been developed and I found a builder prepared to learn how to install them. My tiny, yet costly 7 metre square cottage was started. It would fall far short of its predecessor but it was with great joy in September 2012 that I walked along Barry's brick porch and stepped in through my new front door.

Now the forest resounds with the buzz of my circular saw and my hammering and the kookaburras laugh as I build planter boxes, erect garden arches and surround the cottage in a sea of daisies, lavender and forget-me-nots. I built a bus shelter beside the bunker and the stairs-to-nowhere now connect to the new cottage via a small raised boardwalk.

Recently I began transitioning to retirement. I took up art classes, joined the local writing group and am travelling again. I still go to the opera and the theatre but now attend matinees to avoid being out after dark.

Kylie had told me that 'You can't go back,' and she was right. I have created a new life now. It still centres on Barry but it is a life of my own making. Sometimes I'm lonely but on occasions so is everyone, regardless of their situation – and I have the most wonderful memories to sustain me. I have learned to do a great many things that I would never have considered possible before 2009, and in so doing I have learned a great deal about myself and about people in general.

My days at Waldene are joyful and peaceful and I know that I have come a long way since Black Saturday. Barry is always with me and I am grateful for every day that we had together.

On the six-year anniversary of his loss I received a card from my brother. It said 'We are in awe of your courage and strength to move forward without forgetting.' Perhaps that says it all.

After the fires, Kinglake
She is keeping the bricked verandah
She sweeps it clear of leaves
These grey stains
Are where the window glass melted
Onto the bricks
She is keeping it clear of leaves
Nature is cheerful here
The trees thronging back
Head-high already
After less than two years
Bright leaves dress the black trunks
And the small creek is singing its stones again
It is all that is left of the house
She unfolds a chair on the bricks
Above the valley hazed with burnt trees
And the air resounds
With his heartbeat, his loss
She is sweeping the brick verandah
She is keeping it clear of leaves

– Pam Schindler, January 2011

www.ingramcontent.com/pod-product-compliance
Lightning Source LLC
Chambersburg PA
CBHW032031290426
44110CB00012B/756